2/04

D1377121

Outdoor Weddings

UNFORGETTABLE CELEBRATIONS IN STORYBOOK SETTINGS

by **Mallory Samson**

Text by Mary Duffy

CHRONICLE BOOKS
SAN FRANCISCO

Copyright © 2004 by Mallory Samson. All rights reserved.
No part of this book may be reproduced in any form
without written permission from the publisher.

Library of Congress Cataloging-in-Publication Data:
Samson, Mallory.
Outdoor weddings : unforgettable celebrations in
storybook settings/ By Mallory Samson.
p. cm.
ISBN 0-8118-4020-4
1. Weddings—Planning. I. Title.
HQ745 .S25 2004
395.2'2—dc21
2002154042

Manufactured in Hong Kong

Design by Distinc

Distributed in Canada by
Raincoast Books
9050 Shaughnessy Street
Vancouver, British Columbia V6P 6E5

10 9 8 7 6 5 4 3 2 1

Chronicle Books LLC
85 Second Street
San Francisco, California 94105

www.chroniclebooks.com

To my parents, Helen and John Samson.

Acknowledgments

Like planning a wedding, creating a book requires a team effort, and *Outdoor Weddings* would not have been possible without the support and guidance of the following people: Mikyla Bruder, my editor, whose creative vision was so important to this project; Anne Bunn, who first saw the need for a book about outdoor weddings; Mary Duffy and Tremen Fenner, who assisted me through every stage; and Armand Eisen, for his expert advice.

Thanks also to Leslie Davisson of Chronicle Books, the design team at Chronicle, and Thierry Chantrel, Melinda Dixon, Patti Flowers, Toni Marion, Chris McDonald, Matt Murphy, Melissa Paul, Grant Rector, and Cheryl Stair for sharing their expertise.

And finally, a very special thank you to the brides and grooms who so graciously shared the stories and photographs of such a personal event in their lives.

Contents

Kiri and Doug, page 77

Introduction

Not long ago, only the free-spirited opted for outdoor weddings, and these were generally laid-back, low-cost affairs. No longer. Whether lavish or low-key, more and more weddings are set against a gorgeous backdrop provided by Mother Nature, with ceremonies as varied in size, formality, religious affiliation, and financial investment as those held indoors.

Take bride, groom, and officiant; mix well with family and friends; add drinks, dinner, and dancing, and you've got the usual formula for a wedding. But nature changes the equation—not confined by four walls, creativity has no ceiling, and the weddings in this book are a testament to that. With guest counts ranging from 13 to 300, these pages feature weddings set in vineyards and gardens, in fields and backyards, on beaches and near mountains, at ranches and clubs. In addition to more traditional nuptials, there are some mixed-faith, same-sex, and repeat ceremonies. And everywhere there are contrasts: formally dressed guests lounging in Adirondack chairs, an elegant sit-down dinner in the perfect Frisbee-throwing field, and an intimate service held in an expansive setting.

Weddings are about connections—to tradition, family, home, and, for those pictured here, nature. The symbolism of launching a life together in the outside world, grounded by family and love, and surrounded by natural beauty, is important to the couples you'll meet in this book. Standing on a mesa and admiring a land painted with a breathtaking range of reds, the justice of the peace at Dan de Serpa's and Julie Brown's wedding declared, "We are in God's cathedral."

While this book is filled with beautiful photographs of wedding ceremonies and portraits of radiant couples, it also deals with practicalities, offering tips about everything from organizing a destination ceremony, to choosing a catering company, to dealing with a rainy forecast.

Indeed, weather is always an issue in planning an outdoor wedding, and for a number of the couples, rain, heat, or wind factored into their wedding tales. "There is the excitement in the gamble involved with depending on what nature throws your way, weather-wise," says Sam Hamilton, whose wedding is featured here. "You're simultaneously at the mercy of nature and in cahoots with it."

These weddings offer glorious backdrops, inspired details, and a few cautionary tales. They range from intimate, family-only affairs to lavish gatherings for hundreds. What they have in common is this: each beautifully succeeded in personalizing one of the most universal of events by celebrating in concert with nature.

9

–1–

In Harmony with Nature

A lush garden surrounded by vineyards … a landscape washed in
a painter's palette of colors … mighty oaks and blazing fall foliage …
a turquoise-and-coral-jeweled island. These varied settings inspired the wedding
ceremonies, decorations, and receptions on the pages that follow.

A Day of
Wine & Roses

Candace Brown & Charles Nelson

Candace Brown lived all over the world before settling down in San Francisco with Charles Nelson. When the couple became engaged, she longed for a backyard wedding. That seemed a little impractical, however, for an apartment-dwelling couple whose parents lived in Oklahoma and Bangkok. So they decided to explore California's wine country, their favorite weekend destination, for a place to hold their wedding.

After an exhausting day touring gardens and vineyards, they pulled up to the Beltane Ranch on the suggestion of a friend. The front yard was a profusion of warm-colored flowers leading to a late-nineteenth-century house with wraparound porches on two levels. They followed the aroma of snickerdoodle cookies into a sitting room to meet the manager. They immediately felt at home.

While the architecture had a strong flavor of New Orleans, the setting—overlooking olive groves and vineyards and framed by the rolling hills of Sonoma Valley—reminded the couple of the French countryside. After getting a tour of the grounds and learning that they could have the run of the ranch for their weekend celebration, Charles and Candace got started making their fantasy backyard wedding a reality. They had nine months to plan.

In describing the style of wedding she wanted, Candace would tell friends that it had to be "whimsical and eclectic." She pictured a wedding filled with bright, warm colors to suit her vibrant personality. The ranch's landscape was well suited to her color scheme, with a riot of pinks and oranges in its gardens.

While striving for a relaxed wedding—the guest list was limited to 100 friends and family members—the couple was, by their own admission, very particular about the details. Having been to more than a dozen weddings in the past year, Charles and Candace had a pretty good sense of what was standard and what was outstanding, and they wanted every element of their wedding to carry special meaning. They had become engaged in Paris, so they wanted their celebration to be infused with the flavor of France. Since they were getting married in the Sonoma Valley, where people have adopted a French sensibility about the appreciation of good food and wine, it was a seamless integration.

They were especially discerning when hiring vendors. They started with the Beltane Ranch's recommendations and also tapped into a network of newly married couples. "Friends and relatives would refer us to friends of theirs who had just gotten married.

Everyone was so willing to talk about their weddings, giving us advice and suggesting who to work with and who not to," says Candace. In the end, they were able to build a personal relationship with every vendor they hired. And that kind of communication, says Charles, kept planning difficulties to a minimum.

After securing the Beltane Ranch, they turned their attention to selecting a photographer. "So many people I know put everything into planning their wedding and having this amazing day and then they skimped on the photographer," says Candace. Hiring a person who could capture the feeling of the wedding was, to Charles and Candace, a way to ensure that the memories of the day would be properly preserved.

Six months before the wedding, the location, photographer, caterer, florist, and band had all been lined up, and the couple was debating whether or not to hire a wedding coordinator. Since they had already made the big decisions and hired all the vendors, they wondered if it would be a waste of money. In the end, they decided to get a coordinator who would handle the last-minute details. According to Charles, it was one of the best decisions they made. Not only did the wedding coordinator handle minutiae like what size

Beltane's rustic truck offers guests a welcome sight.

linens to rent, she also helped orchestrate the weekend activities, which began with a wine tasting on Friday afternoon and ended with a Krispy Kreme and espresso breakfast on Sunday morning. Most importantly, says Charles, by having someone to act as maestro, they could savor every moment of their wedding day without being distracted by mundane matters.

The day of their August wedding was glorious, mild and sunny, the air sweet with the fragrance of the gardens. Propped up in the back of the Beltane's rustic pickup truck was a chalkboard reading "Bienvenue" to welcome guests. While waiting for the ceremony to begin, everyone was served lemonade and iced tea. Afraid the temperature might soar, Candace and Charles had provided wooden fans, but these were used more for dramatic effect than heat relief.

As everyone was seated, Charles stood in front of an ivy-covered yellow shed shaded by sprawling oaks. Colorful dahlias in old sap buckets had been hung on the trees. The crowd became still as the bridal attendants walked down the aisle. Their two-piece sheaths were made from Thai silk, the bridesmaids' dresses in tangerine, the maid of honor's in hot pink. Charles and his groomsmen wore box-weave ties in shades that matched the women's outfits.

With music wafting from the upper porch, Candace descended the stairs, escorted by her father, and proceeded down the aisle past family and friends. As if by design, the guests were dressed in a garden array of bright colors, in harmony with the bride's bouquet of pink, orange, and yellow roses. Candace wore a silk scoop-neck dress with spaghetti straps—beautiful but uncomplicated, and perfect for the setting. She wore her hair swept up in soft curls and gentle waves. When she reached Charles, they locked eyes and the ceremony began.

After the ceremony, guests were directed toward one side of the house, where they mingled and sampled hot and cold hors d'oeuvres, served with local wines. Everyone was asked to inscribe a bottle of champagne, the couple's version of a guest book. In return, they were promised an invitation to Charles' and Candace's tenth wedding anniversary, to pop the cork and celebrate again. Nearby,

a mini Eiffel Tower held place cards directing guests to tables, each named for a Parisian landmark.

For the reception, an intimate dining area had been tucked into a clearing protected by ancient oaks and surrounded by vines. The tables were draped in white with a leaf-patterned overlay, while the floral centerpieces were an explosion of color. Throughout dinner, the tableau changed with the light. As the sun set, the sky picked up the warm orange and hot pink color scheme. As night fell, the scene was lit by lanterns in the trees, chunky candles on the table, votive lights along pathways, and twinkling white fairy lights strung along the porch and around the bandstand.

Under other circumstances, after a sumptuous dinner in such an idyllic setting, guests might be lulled into a somniferous state. Not a chance at this event! About fifty yards from the dining area, a picket fence outlined a band shell and dance area lit for the occasion. A rousing zydeco band began playing, and everyone hit the dance floor. A county ordinance prohibits amplified music after 10:00 P.M., so when the hour approached, the band "unplugged" and played on, with Charles trying his hand on the spoons.

"We couldn't have asked for a better day," the groom reports, his new wife smiling in agreement.

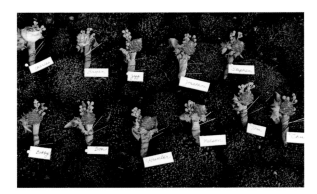

A line of boutonnieres tagged and ready to be pinned.

1.

2.

1. After months of planning,
   Charles and Candace say
   their "I do's."
2. A miniature Eiffel Tower
   doubles as a place-card holder.

1. A vine-patterned overlay dresses the table for the outdoor setting.
2. Roses pick up the warm shade of the bridesmaid's dress.
3. Charles plants a post-ceremony kiss on his new wife.
4. Simple and delicious, the lemon and chocolate wedding cake.

5. The bride and groom take Marie Antoinette literally.
6. Guests dine beneath the sprawling oaks, the perfect place to watch the glorious sunset.

5.

A giant oak tree is
brightened up with
sap buckets overflowing
with color.

Facing the Elements

Candace Brown's natural look was achieved with the help of makeup artist Chris McDonald and hairstylist Toni Marion. The Bay Area duo offers these tips for a picture-perfect look for an outdoor wedding:

• Sunscreen reflects light, so it makes skin appear one or two shades lighter than normal. On the day of the wedding, even though you'll be outdoors, skip the sunscreen.

• Be sure to wear sunscreen *before* your wedding day, however. Overly tanned or sunburned skin is less translucent and less flattering in photographs.

• To hide strap lines that might be visible on your shoulders, arms, or back, use a tattoo cover-up the day of, or a little self-tanner the night before, the wedding.

• When it comes to makeup, less is more. Go for warmer colors and use a light hand with application.

• For striking eyes, start with well-groomed brows and add a few fake lashes.

• Rice paper blotting sheets (available at beauty supply stores) are great for touch-ups on hot days, to absorb sweat while leaving just a touch of powder. Chinese fans can also come in handy just before a walk down the aisle.

• Don't fight the character of your hair. For instance, don't have curly hair straightened—or straight hair curled—that day, as wind and humidity will work against it. Keeping your hair natural looking will give your photographs a timeless quality.

• The best hairstyles for an outdoor event are simple and off the face.

• Hold off on drinks until after photographs have been taken. Alcohol tends to make noses red and skin pink.

• When meeting with a hairstylist or makeup artist, come with swatches of material or a photograph of your wedding dress. Choose someone who will listen to you, someone you feel totally at ease with. You want a person who will help you relax—not add stress—those last few hours before the wedding.

• Do a run-through with both hair and makeup ahead of time to be sure you'll be happy with your look.

• For a successful natural look, select makeup and hairstyles that accent your essential beauty, with a bit more polish.

1.

2.

1. **Pre-wedding bridal attire.**
2. **Time for a quick touch-up.**

21

A Ceremony at
Ghost Ranch

Julie Brown & Dan de Serpa

This was the most intimate of weddings in the most expansive of settings. The striking Southwestern landscape that has inspired so many painters served as the dramatic backdrop for Julie Brown's and Dan de Serpa's wedding. A mesa of red rocks touched the mercurial sky, which, in the course of a couple of hours, changed from deep blue to golden yellow, flaming orange, and finally dusky violet. The red earth stood in for a red carpet, while the bride was a cloud of white amid the colorful surroundings.

Enveloped by the magnificence of the land and the warmth of their families, the bride and groom exchanged vows. Once the couple was declared husband and wife, accordionists struck up a tune. Then the wedding party of a dozen drove a short way to a log cabin for champagne, grapes, caviar, foie gras, pretzels, and popcorn.

Julie and Dan had always wanted nature to play an important role in their wedding ceremony. Living in Northern California, they had many outdoor venues to choose among and explored beaches, vineyards, and mountaintops. But while each was beautiful, none resonated with the couple. Then Julie learned that Ghost Ranch, the property where Georgia O'Keeffe once lived and painted, was

1. An accordion player adds
   to the festivities.
2. Family and friends gather
   for the ceremony.

24

available to the public, and her heart soared. "Her paintings have always spoken to me," says Julie. Two months before the wedding, she headed to New Mexico, knowing she would return with her wedding site secured.

After checking out a few spots in Santa Fe, Julie and a friend headed 100 miles northwest to Ghost Ranch, now a conference center run by the Presbyterian Church. While the ranch encompasses some 20,000 acres, the buildings are clustered together in a 5-acre patch. As they were being shown around, a guide suggested that the apple orchard might serve as a good place for the ceremony. But, since it was surrounded by buildings, in clear sight of a parking lot, it was not what the bride-to-be had in mind. After getting hiking recommendations, Julie and her friend went off to explore the unpopulated areas of the ranch.

They drove to the end of a dirt road and started walking. Within five minutes they came to a majestic area bordered by red and yellow cliffs and dusted with low-lying shrubbery, with an uninterrupted landscape. Depending on the direction one faces, the terrain changes with hints of the valley and canyons beyond. The setting is spectacular in its raw beauty and quiet as a church, a place where adornment would be superfluous. Julie and her friend turned to each other and said, "This is the spot."

On their way back to the conference center, the women discovered a small log cabin. The exterior was a shell, the inside a dirt floor and nothing more. They learned that the cabin was built as part of the set for the movie *City Slickers*. Now, with the right props, it would be the perfect spot for post-ceremony hors d'oeuvres. "We wanted to keep the wedding relaxed, with just our immediate families, and we didn't want to spend a lot of money," says Julie. "But I cared very much about the aesthetics of everything."

The location in place, Julie headed back to Santa Fe to iron out various details. The guests—all twelve of them—would arrive on a Saturday, and the wedding would be held on Monday in the late afternoon. Julie found a restaurant for the rehearsal dinner, another for the reception, and a hotel where they could all stay. On the prowl for weekend activities that would bring both families

2.

together, she took a test run on a sunset train ride that included a barbecue and campfire, and added that to the wedding weekend itinerary. She also took note of a farmers' market where she could pick up flowers to place in the guests' rooms. At dinner her last night in town, Julie met a very personable waiter. Later she called and asked if he would be the server for their rustic log cabin cocktail party.

Back in San Francisco, Julie enlisted a designer friend to create her bridal gown. She wanted a dress that fit her sense of beauty: simple yet striking. With her input, her friend fashioned a gown with a crushed-velvet bodice, silk spaghetti straps, and full skirt of embroidered tulle. He also made a shawl, using the velvet material. Surrounded by rugged beauty, Julie would be an ethereal bride standing on terra firma.

Five days before the wedding, Julie and Dan flew to New Mexico. Her parents, meanwhile, had opted to drive and loaded their car with a table, Mexican blankets, vases, candles, and other decorative touches to set the stage for the post-wedding cocktail hour, plus a cooler full of ingredients for hors d'oeuvres, before embarking from San Francisco.

When it came to choosing the music to celebrate their marriage, the couple skirted convention by booking an accordionist. It was the instrument Dan's father had played, and they chose this way to honor his memory.

By Saturday afternoon all the guests had arrived. As Julie had hoped, the sunset train ride proved a perfect way to introduce the two families. At a flea market on Sunday, the bride and groom crossed the last few items off their wedding to-do list: they picked up mother-of-pearl cufflinks for Dan and turquoise wedding rings for each other.

The morning of the wedding, the couple awoke to overcast skies, and Julie remembered the guide at Ghost Ranch warning that it rained every September afternoon. At the time she had been certain her wedding day would defy the odds with nothing but sunshine; now she wondered whether she should have taken the guide's advice and secured an indoor location in case of rain. But she quickly decided that rain or shine, the weather wasn't going to put a damper on the day.

Meanwhile, Julie's sister and mother took charge of the floral arrangements, using the colors of the landscape for inspiration. For the bride they designed a bouquet of yellow and red roses, interspersed with berries and peppercorns and tied with a thick satin ribbon. For the groom's boutonniere, they chose a golden rose tinged in red. To dress up the porch of the log cabin, they filled a cast-iron bucket with a loose arrangement of the same flowers, long stemmed and uncut. When they finished, it was time to head to Ghost Ranch.

At 4:30 P.M., Julie, escorted by her father, walked down the red clay aisle to join Dan at their outdoor altar. The groom, overwhelmed by the sight of his bride in the glorious surroundings,

began to cry. Julie, on the other hand, radiated peace as the two were declared husband and wife.

The ceremony complete, the wedding party made their way to the log cabin just as nature began acting out, kicking up a windstorm. Fortified with champagne and tasty hors d'oeuvres the guests huddled for thirty minutes until the dust settled. Then, for the first time all day, the clouds broke and the sun cast a warm glow. Delighted by the fanciful cocktail party, relatives laughed and chatted until it was time to head back for the final event on the wedding schedule, dinner in the wine room at the historic El Dorado hotel.

While everyone piled into cars for the ride back to Santa Fe, the newly married couple lingered, basking in a showy sunset and their love of each other. Driving to the hotel, they watched the light show until the sun finally set, taking with it all the fiery brilliance of the afternoon.

Reflecting on the day, Julie says, "Our wedding was always about being surrounded by the people we love most, in a beautiful setting to demonstrate our love of nature, and that's exactly what we did. We loved our wedding."

As the ceremony begins, the judge declares, "We are in God's Cathedral."

The radiant bride takes in the
magnificent surroundings.

1. A post-wedding toast.
2. Who needs fois gras when you have peanut butter and jelly?
3. A flower-filled bucket adds a decorative touch to the cabin.

4. Dan and Julie enjoy a quiet walk.
5. The sister of the bride prepared
   for a change in weather.
6. Wedding party poses for a picture.

4.

5.

6.

29

1.

Picture Perfect

Julie wanted an aesthetically pleasing wedding and chose a background that was camera-ready. The results are beautiful memories and striking photographs that will last a lifetime. The bride, a one-time model, suggests, "Hire a photographer you trust, discuss the pictures you want taken, then let her do her job." Here are some other tips for ensuring that the photographs capture the best of the day:

- Take advantage of the light when it is at its most beautiful. The most flattering pictures are those taken about an hour (or hour and a half) before the sun disappears.

- When hiring a photographer, talk about the timing of the ceremony and reception to make sure it corresponds with the light. Ask your photographer to meet with you and check out possible backdrops for pictures before the wedding and discuss options for inclement weather.

- If the sunlight is harsh or the background is all greenery, photographs shot in black and white will be softer and more flattering.

- When planning family and group pictures, think about a setting where relatives will be comfortable. Asking your eighty-five-year-old grandmother to traipse through the dunes might not be the best choice.

- If the bride or groom wears glasses, make sure they have nonreflective lenses.

- Ask your wedding party to dispense with sunglasses during the picture-taking portion of the wedding.

1. A Mexican blanket becomes the perfect table covering.
2. The former movie set becomes the picture perfect location for cocktails.
3. Julie's bouquet reflects the fiery colors of the setting.
4. The groom savors the moment.

Nature & Nurture

Francesca Vietor & Mark Hertsgaard

The attendants wore Wellingtons, the guests carried umbrellas, and the bride's gown was trimmed in mud. Nature provided some high drama for Francesca Vietor's and Mark Hertsgaard's wedding. The bride and groom have made careers promoting the protection of the environment—she as an activist, he as a writer—and they wanted their wedding to be a celebration of both their love for each other and their connection to the earth. And it was. But the beautiful Indian summer day that they had envisioned, with fall foliage blazing and nature shining in all its glory, wasn't to be.

Instead, it rained—and rained, and rained—until the site of the ceremony, near an oak tree at the edge of a lagoon, was too miry to walk on. Luckily, two days earlier, the couple had reserved a tent, just in case, so the nuptials were moved under cover. Guests wouldn't get to hike to and from the ceremony on the trails that had been carefully cleared of poison oak and marked with floral arrangements. And the wind and rain meant forgoing such whimsical touches as a canoe filled with flowers, an altar made from hay bales, and strings of sparkling lights in the trees. But these things hardly mattered.

Just in time for the 4:00 P.M. ceremony, the rain stopped, the sides of the tent were pulled back, and as if on cue, birds began to sing. A little later, the crackling of not-too-distant thunder added to nature's soundtrack.

Francesca had spent the night at a cottage a short distance from the wedding spot. About an hour before the ceremony, she slipped into her wedding gown, a silk organza scoop-necked dress, fitted to the hips and flared in the skirt. It had a short train and at the lower back, a cluster of silk flowers, the colors of persimmon and cranberry. The bride arrived via four-wheeler, the only vehicle that could make it up the muddy trail. The car pulled right next to the cottage, and with the help of the driver, the bride's feet—and dress—never touched the ground.

As a violinist, flutist, and guitarist played, the processional started. The officiating minister, the friend who had introduced Mark and Francesca, was first down the aisle. He had become, by virtue of the Internet, an ordained minister when the couple asked him to marry them. The very personal, nontraditional ceremony acknowledged loved ones who had passed away, including Francesca's parents, paid homage to the earth with the planting of an oak tree, and reflected the couple's commitment to each other through vows they had written themselves. The rings were presented in a pumpkin carved with their initials, carried by the three-year-old son of a friend.

After the ceremony, which took place on a friend's farm in Northern California, guests headed up the hill to a porch, where they took the edge off the chill with black currant vodka martinis and hors d'oeuvres. As afternoon turned to evening, everyone moved into the barn, which was cozy and warm, golden with candlelight and decorated in warm autumnal colors. A pair of large votive-candle chandeliers hung from the ceiling, and the out-of-doors had been lovingly brought inside with greenery, flowers, fruits of the fall harvest, and foliage-colored decorations. The tables were topped with pumpkin-colored linens, copper-colored china, and candleholders made from fallen oak branches. When the bride first walked into the barn, she began to cry. "I thought it was amazing

1. **Mementos for the guests—burlap-wrapped saplings for future planting.**
2. **The canoe sits unused due to an unexpected rainstorm.**
3. **A sign of the couple's love of nature.**

1.

2.

3.

and magical, with all the seasonal colors. It had a tonal quality that was so beautiful," she remembers.

Upstairs in the hayloft, meanwhile, it was Halloween heaven for the kids. Their exclusive domain included tables filled with plenty of treats, pumpkins, and creepy-crawlers. As the party of around 130 guests got rolling and the adults were starting to hit the dance floor, the kids were hanging gummy bears, flowers, toy spiders, and anything else they could string together from the rafters.

At every stage of the planning phase, Mark and Francesca had worked together to ensure that their wedding would reflect their value system. "There can be so much waste involved in putting together a wedding, from the invitations to the gifts. We thought about the ecological and social implications of every detail," Francesca explains. They sent out invitations on hemp paper printed with soy-based inks. The carrot seedling place cards were plantable. "We wanted to help educate people that these items exist," continues Francesca. All the food and even the wine came from surrounding farms and vineyards, and most was organically grown. At the end of the celebration, leftovers were donated to a food bank or composted.

The oak tree was central to the theme of Mark's and Francesca's wedding. The site was named Oak Mesa, and centuries ago, the acorn had been incorporated into the Vietor family crest. The couple also appreciated the metaphor of an acorn taking root and growing into a mighty oak. So, acorns and oak leaves adorned the wedding cake and were included in the floral arrangements, the groom's boutonniere, and the bride's bouquet. Besides presenting each guest with a sapling to plant, the couple says, "We also asked people not to give us gifts, but instead to support two tree-planting groups."

While they were very conscientious during the planning stages, in the barn on their wedding day, it was time to celebrate. And the weather certainly didn't put a damper on anything. In fact, Francesca says, she wouldn't have changed even that. "It was so dramatic and cozy and different. It demonstrated the power of Mother Nature in the truest sense."

**Extreme weather calls for
extreme footwear.**

1. Husks hold seeds for guests
   to throw after the ceremony.
2. Pumpkins and roses, central
   to the wedding decor.

1.

2.

1.

2.

1. Inclement weather couldn't
   dampen the spirit of the
   wedding.
2. A tableau befitting a farm.
3. The happy bride and groom.
4. Foliage and flowers adorn the
   wedding cake.

3.

4.

5. Oak candlesticks light up
   a table.
6. The homemade guest book.

Nature in all its beauty.

Weather or Not

As Francesca and Mark discovered, when preparing for an outdoor wedding, it pays to have a backup plan. Think it through carefully— a contingency scenario may become a wedding reality. A few just-in-case tips:

- In planning your outdoor wedding, prepare yourself emotionally for the possibility of bad weather.
- Having a tent on hold—as Mark and Francesca did—or an alternative indoor location is key for protection against the elements.
- Stock up on umbrellas if the weather forecast is iffy.
- Rain isn't the only weather concern. You may want portable air conditioners or heaters on standby in case the mercury dips or soars.

- If the walkways or parking areas at the wedding site are primarily dirt, have mulch on hand in case of rain, to keep mud at bay.
- Talk to your photographer about an inclement weather alternative for picture-taking.
- For about $200, a wedding insurance policy can offer financial protection in case the wedding has to be postponed due to worst-case scenarios, such as sickness, injury, or extreme weather conditions.

1. A hollowed-out pumpkin holds the wedding rings.
2. The flower girl dressed in wedding white.

A Wedding

By the Sea

Madzy Besselaar & Ian Taylor

The barefoot bride descended the cliffside staircase and waited for her cue to walk down a daisy-lined aisle. Water the color of turquoise jewels outshined the blue of the sky. A breeze strong enough to blow the hair in your eyes but gentle enough to leave the sand in its place kept the sunny day temperate. White-capped waves crashed a safe distance away from the rows of white chairs, then gently rolled to shore. Eighty family members and friends had traveled to this paradise in Bermuda to attend the wedding of Madzy Besselaar and Ian Taylor.

The wedding site was nestled in a shell-shaped cove, the surrounding limestone cliffs deflecting the wind. Madzy's little nieces and nephews—girls dressed in lemon-colored organza dresses and flower wreaths, boys in white shirts and seersucker shorts—amused guests as they made their way down the aisle leaving a trail of flower petals. The bride was in "beach formal," a scoop-neck organza dress embroidered with flowers, fitted on top and flared at the bottom. Her loosely tied bouquet of lilies of the valley and hydrangeas was predominantly white, accented with turquoise to match the trim on her bridesmaids' watery-blue dresses. They carried pink-and-white bouquets tied with turquoise

1. **The bride and groom lead the recessional.**
2. **The sea and sand provide a dramatic backdrop.**

ribbon. The wedding party looked even more beautiful as the afternoon sun began casting a pink light over the beach.

As a violinist and flutist played, Madzy, flanked by her parents, made her way to a tulle-and-bamboo huppah to stand beside Ian. He was dressed for the tropics in light-colored pants, tan jacket, and sea-colored shirt. While most of the guests and wedding party could feel the sand between their toes, the groom kept his shoes on, prepared to participate in the traditional glass-breaking at the conclusion of the ceremony. Reciting vows they had written, the couple was pronounced husband and wife by the bride's seventh-grade religion teacher.

When Madzy and Ian first became engaged, they thought about a number of possible wedding scenarios, including eloping. "I'm not a big center-of-attention person," says Madzy. The thought of walking down a long aisle in a big church wedding terrified the bride-to-be. But the couple decided that they wanted to enter married life surrounded by family and friends, and her parents' home in Bermuda was the natural choice for a setting. They both loved the island, they couldn't ask for a more scenic backdrop, and the relaxed atmosphere of a beach wedding suited their style.

Madzy grew up in New Jersey, Ian in Minnesota, and they now lived in Seattle. Their guest list included friends and family from all over the United States and Europe. From the start, the couple was concerned that the expense of traveling to a resort island would be hard for some to manage, so they went out of their way to find accommodations in every price range. There were twenty other weddings taking place in Bermuda that same weekend, which added to the challenge. Luckily, some neighboring friends of the family graciously offered the use of their homes for wedding guests.

As soon as the date was set, Madzy and Ian sent out a save-the-date card, to ensure ample time for booking flights. They also established a wedding Web site, which kept guests informed about everything from the weather forecast to the weekend itinerary. Although they invited some 130, Ian and Madzy had no idea how many guests to plan for until they received the response cards. As it turned out, 80 made the trip.

From the start, Madzy had a very clear vision of what she wanted and decided to forgo having a wedding planner. She envisioned a beachside ceremony, followed by a reception in the yard under a tent canopy, with mesmerizing ocean views. The beach influenced

45

Feet firmly planted in
the sand, Madzy and Ian
exchange vows.

1. Flower girls armed with petal-filled baskets.
2. A bottle holds treasures from the sea, as well as the wedding program.
3. The ring bearer in his Bermuda best.
4. The perfect setting for a memorable seaside wedding.

1.

2.

4.

3.

The tables reflect the
colors of the sea.

A bridesmaid's bouquet.

every aspect of the wedding plans, from the stationery—the invitations were in deep blue script on silvery blue paper; the programs, sand colored with ocean-blue lettering—to the table decorations, which included seashells. White-and-blue patterned china sat atop silky, white embroidered linens. Candles floating in round glass vases lined with sand and seashells added to the tropical mood. Bath salts in silk sachets presented in light blue boxes were given to guests as a favor. The floral arrangements of tulips, roses, and hydrangeas were blue and white with touches of purple and orange.

While Madzy had strong opinions about the flowers and the overall decor, she deferred to her mother when it came to choosing the caterer and a menu for the sit-down dinner. (Her father chose the wine, a special vintage from his own collection.) As it turned out, the experience of planning the wedding proved to be an opportunity for mother-daughter bonding. "My mother and I were completely on the same page," says Madzy. She and Ian went to Bermuda once during the planning stage, but they handled most of the details long-distance. "The four-hour time difference was sometimes a problem," she says, but luckily her parents spent a lot of time there and were able to work closely with local vendors on behalf of the couple.

Madzy and Ian were determined to personalize their wedding as much as possible. They wanted it to be both beautiful and meaningful, with original vows and touches like handmade programs-in-a-bottle. Choosing the music for the ceremony took some time. While at work, Madzy listened to popular wedding compilations and hours of classical music before coming up with the pieces she wanted.

Madzy and Ian don't think of their wedding as the culmination of months of planning, but rather as the launching of their life together. "You can't get so wrapped up in details that you lose sight of that," says Madzy. "For five years we'd been together, and we had gone through so much, and just getting to this place was an amazing feat, and that's what we wanted to celebrate."

The bride and groom arrived in Bermuda the Tuesday before their wedding with their work cut out for them. They still had

programs and favors to assemble and welcome baskets to deliver to guests' hotels. (Besides the weekend itinerary and maps of the island, the baskets contained Bermuda rum and treats including chocolate, cheese, and crackers.) Fortunately, they had help. Madzy's sister and sister-in-law framed pictures with the names and images of island flora and hung them on the pillars of the pool pavilion. Madzy's father was the transportation expert, arranging shuttles to and from each event. Keeping track of who was arriving when and the number of guests for each pre-wedding activity was a challenge, and an unforeseen taxi strike made his job a bit more difficult.

On the day of the wedding, friends were enlisted for beach duty: raking sand, picking up litter, and arranging chairs. Meanwhile, at the house, aunts and other relatives were pitching in to set tables and arrange flowers and candles. At 10:30 A.M., Madzy retired as wedding coordinator and became a bride. She took a long walk to relax, then went to have her nails, hair, and makeup done.

After the ceremony, guests left the beach and headed back up the stairs to the Besselaars' home. A breathtaking scene awaited them as they walked through the house toward the poolside cocktail area. "It was like walking into heaven with all the flowers and decorations," says Madzy. The porch, pool, and tent were lit with dozens of candles. There were Chinese paper lanterns hanging from the trees and inside the tent, floating candles on the tabletops, and even orchids floating in the pool. As night began to fall, ground lights illuminated the pathways.

From an upper porch, the band played as guests enjoyed the sushi bar, nibbled on hors d'oeuvres, drank martinis, and sampled Madzy's favorite tropical drink, the mojito. Before heading to the dinner tent, everyone joined the couple at the side of house, where a heart-shaped hole had been dug. As is the custom in Bermuda, the happy couple planted a cedar tree.

The wedding day ended with a bit of Bermuda magic: late that night, as the reception wound to a close, a chorus of tree frogs serenaded the guests. "We had this beautiful humming coming from the trees. It was music we didn't have to pay for!" says Madzy.

1. Guests mingle beside
   the reception tent.
2. The beach bride keeps
   it simple.
3. Husband and wife take
   a quiet moment.

2.

1.

3.

4. The ring bearers study
   a bouquet.
5. A row of daisies line the aisle.

4.

5.

Bowls containing seashells
and floating candles add to
the table decor.

Surf, Sand, and Ceremony

A wedding on the beach can be scenic, romantic, and memorable, but some planning is in order. A few tips:

- Check the tide schedule. Low tide can bring beach residue and a smell that's less than pleasant. With high tides come the threat of rogue waves. Madzy planned her ceremony for an ebb, or outgoing, tide because the surf is usually quieter as it works its way out.
- Be sure to have a crew on hand the day of the wedding for raking the beach and setting the scene.
- Beach breezes can be refreshing, but they can also wreak havoc on floral arrangements and other decorations. Keep everything simple and well anchored.
- The wind can send a short veil sailing, so consider going with a longer style.
- Wind also affects acoustics. Look for a cove buffered by rock, as Madzy and Ian did.

- If you are planning to use a public beach, check with local officials to see if a permit is necessary (also check to see whether alcohol is permitted).
- Now, for the obvious: unless you're a gambler, you might not want to schedule a beach wedding during hurricane season.
- Even if you've chosen the driest month, have a backup plan for bad weather.

1. Paper lanterns add color and light to the tent.
2. A daisy accents the menu card.

—2—

Setting the Stage

Sometimes nature plays art director for wedding dreams and themes:
In a vibrant, red-hued tent, a backyard wedding gets everybody talking ...
from a flourishing yard grows an idea—the Greek Isles go Hamptons ...
a California garden inspires a Mediterranean ambience.

Big, Bold &
Beautiful

Alexandra Hynansky & Gene Vados

When friends and family arrived for Alexandra (Lexie) Hynansky's and Gene Vados's wedding reception, they were ushered into an enormous open-sided tent furnished like a living room, with a chandelier here, a chaise there. The theme was white-on-white punctuated by splashes of pale blue, and the tent floor was luxuriously carpeted with Berber rugs. Clusters of café tables and chairs at the back offered additional seating. Hundreds of yards of lush white draping curtained off the back of the tent, and gel lighting and candles added to the overall clean look.

The setting was the home of the bride's parents. Their expansive front lawn easily accommodated three tents, including a long foyer so guests could go from car to tent without stepping on damp ground. The majestic trees that dominated the yard were decked with lanterns, which illuminated the ground with soft spotlights. Three hundred guests, some sinking into well-stuffed couches, others milling about, nibbled on whimsical hors d'oeuvres, such as sushi "cigars" and artichoke "lollipops." A trio of flamenco musicians strolled through the sea of people, who responded with delight.

At the conclusion of the cocktail hour, the massive curtain at the back parted—but the dining area behind was still hidden by fluttering ribbons of silk organza. Lexie wanted to surprise her guests. As they left the room of wedding whites and Tiffany blues, parting the strips of fabric to move into the next tent, there was a collective gasp, followed by oohs and aahs of appreciation as everyone took in the dramatic scene.

The bride-to-be had wanted a statement wedding, big and bold to reflect her personality—pastels wouldn't do; the colors had to be daring. And they were. The room was awash in deep reds, with lacquered chairs, rich tablecloths, and tightly packed bouquets of roses accented by hot pink and turquoise. Throughout the space, stone column pedestals held massive urns full of deep red roses. Tables had smaller arrangements of red and hot pink roses and peonies and were set with white plates topped with white napkins inside napkin holders inscribed in red. The support beams of the enormous tent (100 by 300 feet) were lavishly wrapped in white muslin. On a side table, a seven-tier cake demanded attention. Its intricate mosaic design in gold leaf topped with an urn made it look like a model of Ukrainian architecture, a reference to Lexie's heritage. Dozens of flickering votive candles, together with pink gel lighting, underscored the striking look.

Set to the music of the flamenco players, the room had a decidedly Spanish flair, and Lexie was dressed to match. Her low-back strapless gown of Chantilly lace was form fitting, with an expanse of lace that trailed behind her. Her long black hair was pulled back into a chignon and adorned with a white orchid; drop earrings added to the elegant effect.

As guests acclimated to the dramatic environment, spring salads were served. The rest of the dinner was buffet style, with an eclectic mix of entrees: miso salmon, wild mushroom risotto, and steak frites. Throughout dinner the flamenco players performed, creating an energy that stripped the guests of their inhibitions. When a sixteen-piece band began to play, the crowd was primed to hit the dance floor.

Lexie's wedding-to-remember had been in the planning for ten months. She knew an at-home reception with 300 guests would be an enormously complicated undertaking, so she immediately hired a wedding coordinator. As she says, "You're basically putting together a building from scratch." Luckily, she was able to find someone who could produce an event of that magnitude and wouldn't try to temper her bold vision.

The wedding coordinator handled all the details of interior design and furniture rental. Throughout the months of planning, after conversations about particulars, she would approach Lexie with a few options to choose among. It was a system that worked well. Some big decisions came easily: Lexie definitely wanted a separate tent for cocktails, a tented walkway in case of rain, and flooring throughout. Anything frilly or cutesy was out. Anything tentative was out. Anything that shouted "wedding" was out. Her edict: "I do not want one white lily or any pale pink roses." On the other hand, it took a lot of back and forth before the color scheme of the reception tent was finally decided. Lexie wanted an avant-garde look, so deep red was chosen to create a dramatic effect. Gradually, Lexie and the coordinator added hot pink and turquoise as accent colors.

Bright pink blooms in turquoise containers add a splash of contrasting color.

1.

1. A Bentley drives home the message of the day.
2. The bride in all her glory.

2.

1. Lexie takes one last look
    before the ceremony.
2. A silver tray adds a touch
    of elegance.
3. Soft lighting comes from
    lanterns hanging from
    the trees.

3.

2.

1.

A tented foyer leads to the
cocktail and reception areas.

The color scheme would be carried through to the outfits worn by the bride's attendants. Working with a dressmaker, Lexie helped design raw silk dresses in hot pink and deep rose. The long skirts were slit to the knee and featured a ruffled border. The women were given a choice of six styles of tops to choose from. The flower girl wore the same deep rose as the maid of honor, piped in hot pink. The bride carried an all-white bouquet of roses, peonies, and sweet peas, while her bridesmaids carried bouquets in shades of rose and deep pink.

Lexie also considered the look of her invitations very carefully. She wanted something that would set the tone of the wedding. She went with a luxurious paper stock engraved in gold Italianate script and wrapped in blue tissue. Her father is a car dealer and both she and Gene work in the family business, so she found antique car stamps for the envelopes.

With 300 guests, assigned seating is a must, but Lexie rejected the formality of a sit-down dinner. The wedding coordinator recommended a husband-and-wife catering team known for fanciful dishes, and they collaborated on menus for the hors d'oeuvres and buffet. The father of the bride had one request—that

they hire plenty of bartenders, so guests weren't left standing in line waiting for drinks.

With all of those people—and all that free-flowing alcohol—Lexie made sure the bathrooms they imported were inviting. Trailers were set up away from the party. They were carpeted, scented with candles, decorated with paintings, and filled with cosmetic goodies. One New York City–based friend came back to the reception tent and reported that the bathroom was bigger than her apartment.

In the end, Lexie's attention to detail paid off. "When you're in the middle of planning an outdoor wedding, it seems like it will never come together and you worry about everything from staging to lighting to the draping. But when the day comes, it's definitely worth all the effort," she reports. She got exactly the wedding and reaction she wanted. The people of Wilmington, Delaware, are still talking about it!

Place cards penned with
a flourish.

1. A massive urn holds a vibrant collection of roses.
2. Cake as architecture.
3. Keepsakes for each guest.
4. Hot pink cushions punctuate the deep reds.

**Buckets of champagne
on reserve.**

Planning for the Best

Lexie's wedding was large and elaborate, and she couldn't have undertaken it without a wedding planner who knew her stuff. Melissa Paul certainly does, and she offers the following advice for couples organizing their own outdoor weddings:

- If you decide to hire a wedding planner, speak with them to see if your personalities and taste are compatible, since you'll be spending considerable amounts of time together and trusting them with much of the design and management of your event.

- If appropriate, consider an enclosure card or notation on the reception card inviting guests to attend in "garden attire"—particularly if you expect them to walk long distances or stand for any length of time on grass, dirt, or sand.

- Consult with your rental company to determine what structures are required and where they will be best situated to avoid buried or hanging utility lines and trees, as well as what else would be useful for seasonal comfort, such as heating, air conditioning, or fans.

- Determine what power, staging, lighting, and travel needs are required for musicians or other talent. Many musicians may not want to set instruments on the ground and will require some type of platform.

- When hiring a caterer, make sure to find a company with the ability to serve sophisticated, stylish fare from a field kitchen. Ask if they can provide their own water, ice, power, and ovens or if these will have to be set up for them. Have a designated space for the "kitchen," whether in a shed, garage, or separate tent. Ideally, it will have plenty of access for wait staff and be located near the dining area. A cook tent should be as level as possible and set up with service lighting and power drops for equipment.

- If place cards are to be used, pin them in place or hold them down with a strand of ribbon secured on both ends. Otherwise, all that lovely calligraphy will blow away with one little breeze.

- In addition, determine whether the planner has experience producing outdoor weddings like the one you envision. In a case like Lexie's, the location is basically a construction site requiring hardware—flooring, tenting, lighting, heating, etc.—and interior software such as flowers, draping, and props to create atmosphere. And of course, the planner must be able to assist with standard party elements like music, invitations, and catering.

Lexie and Gene share a kiss.

A Romantic Odyssey

Gina Cambre & Storm Boswick

Gina (Gin) Cambre and Storm Boswick had been married for six years when they decided to have a second wedding. The first had been a simple ceremony at City Hall, and they wanted a more special celebration. Gin had given a lot of thought to what she wanted in a second wedding and amassed magazine articles, pictures, and ideas in a bursting three-ring binder. When the time came to stop collecting and start planning, she was overwhelmed by the endless array of options. With no clear creative direction—other than holding the ceremony outdoors—she knew she needed assistance.

Based on personal recommendations, their good reputations, and her own gut reaction, she hired a florist and wedding coordinator. Over the next eight months, the three engaged in a creative mind-meld, editing ideas, eliminating themes, and sifting through pictures until they had a clear focus for the wedding. The real turning point came when Gin was creating a save-the-date card and invitation. She wanted a design element to formalize the look and leafed through books until she stopped at a drawing of an urn. She decided to use it on all the wedding stationery, and the Grecian theme was set: the Hamptons meet the Greek Isles.

The setting, the couple's flourishing yard, was a showcase of greenery: soaring trees, massive hedges, flowering shrubbery, and an expansive lawn. On one side of the house were neat rows of white chairs; on the other side, a white tent was set for dinner. In the back, clusters of white furniture—beach house formal—and marble tables adorned with flower-filled urns provided a gracious setting for the cocktail hour. Artfully placed Grecian statues, stone and granite columns, screens, and mirrors anchored the theme. Dressed in black and white, as directed, guests became the visual equivalent of a Greek chorus, lending their look to the overall motif.

It took months to find a way to seamlessly integrate the natural majesty of the trees and greenery in the yard with the wedding. "I kept thinking the house would be distracting. I didn't think it would be cohesive," Gin remembers. But in fact, rather than detracting from the scene, the house helped frame the different areas.

Storm, a wine and food connoisseur, took charge in working with the caterer, devising the menu, and selecting the wine. He bought a number of special vintages, so each table could drink a different wine. The night before the wedding, he adjusted the temperature in the wine storage unit, but the next day, he discovered that all the bottles were frozen and starting to explode! So the groom spent the morning of his wedding scouring liquor stores all over the Hamptons. Catastrophe averted, the tables were once again stocked with wine.

Gin and Storm had only recently met the nondenominational minister who would be officiating but quickly grew to trust her judgment. Together they worked to create a ceremony that was spiritual and meaningful, but without an emphasis on traditional religion. The minister recommended books for the couple to look through and helped them assemble their vows. When Gin mentioned that she wanted to address the guests to tell how she had come to fall in love with Storm, and that she was nervous about it, the minister offered to help her work on the delivery. "She was just marvelous," says Gin.

As the sun started to set, the statuesque bride, draped in white silk crepe, headed down the grassy aisle escorted by her mother and Storm's stepfather. She was preceded by eleven bridesmaids, each in a unique white dress and carrying short-stemmed white calla lilies. Storm and Gin stood in a place where the glow of the setting sun reflected on them as they read their vows. They had opted not to have music during the ceremony. Instead, the bride and groom and close family members remembered loved ones who had passed away, including Gin's father, by ringing bells.

After the ceremony, guests moved into the cocktail area, where candlelight glowed in every corner. The black-and-white-clad crowd created a dramatic picture against the backdrop of greenery. After enjoying drinks and hors d'oeuvres, everyone moved to the reception area. The open-sided tent had been situated so branches from bordering trees would naturally hang inside, and rented fig trees were "planted" in the lawn. The table linens, china, candles, and flowers were white, a visual break from all the greenery.

After dinner, a DJ spun records and the dancing began, continuing far into the night until the police arrived to remind the couple of the 11:30 P.M. cutoff time for music. Their Greek Isles wedding was over. The first time around, Gin and Storm had barely been able to afford dinner with friends. This time, they had all that and more in a beautiful setting of their own making.

Soaring trees offer a dramatic backdrop.

Gin and Storm
exchange vows.

1. **Furniture frames the cocktail area.**
2. **A giant fern provides extra greenery.**

2.

3.

4.

3. Bringing the indoors outdoors.
4. Place cards brighten a table.
5. A Norwegian wedding cake, in honor of the groom's heritage.
6. Guests all dressed in black and white.
7. A comfortable couch is a welcomed touch.

7.

6.

5.

1. **A groomsman's boutonniere.**
2. **Stepping out, pirate-style.**
3. **The men's corner.**
4. **Jackets no longer needed.**
5. **The perfect coat rack.**

1.

3.

2.

4.

1. For the bride, a bouquet of long-stemmed calla lilies.
2. Storm and Gin go for a wedding stroll.

Light the Way

At an outdoor reception, the right lighting is imperative, not only for aesthetics but also for safety reasons (in some places, the fire marshal requires pathway lighting). "All of the effort the bride and groom put into the look of the space could have been lost if the tent and surrounding landscape hadn't been lit properly," says Matt Murphy, the lighting designer for Gin's and Storm's wedding. He offers other illuminating tips:

- Lighting can be as simple or dramatic as you wish. At this wedding, a crystal chandelier added drama and sparkle to the tent.
- A soft white light pointed directly over tables can delicately spill light, accenting table decor and flowers. Used with candle light, it gives tables a nice warm glow. With pin spots, if you look throughout the room you will see gentle bursts of ambient light every few feet, which is pleasing to the eye.

- When lighting the interior of a tent, the more subtle the better. Light the perimeter of the tent so the light spills gently up the canopy, and use rose and amber gels for a warm and rosy glow throughout the room.
- An up-light through a full canopy of leaves makes every leaf stand out against a night sky. It's a great contrast of light and dark. For outdoor ceremonies, I sometimes create a subtle moonlight effect using down-lights in the trees.
- Light little nooks and other areas on the property that have character and would normally get lost in the shadows. Up-light any special statues or unique structures for dramatic impact.
- With a large property, light trees at different distances to give the landscape dimension.
- A swimming pool is a fascinating canvas for light, using still or moving projected patterns.

- Paper lanterns add a whimsical touch to any space. They can be giant ones that demand attention or tiny puffs that dangle from slender branches.
- For bartenders or musicians who are working outside and need functional light, use stronger spotlights so that they can see. If there are no trees around, you can install these on a house roof or tall bamboo poles.
- I try to work with the florist to highlight runners, flowers, and so on. Lights can make flowers and foliage pop. Use up-lights on florist's foliage that is wrapped around tent poles; without lights, these look like fuzzy shadows clinging to the poles.
- In a tent, highlight key items with pin spots, such as the wedding cake and the bride-and-groom's table.
- Always set up and check everything the night before, while there's still time to make alterations.
- Overall, subtlety is the most important thing: an outdoor wedding must never look like Times Square!

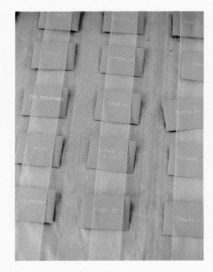

Strips of sheer fabric protect place cards from the wind.

Splendor
In the Grass

Kiri Upsall & Doug Miro

She is from London; he is from Michigan. They met in Paris and lived in Los Angeles. But when it came time to select their wedding location, Kiri Upsall and Doug Miro chose none of the above. They wanted a late-summer outdoor wedding, and unreliable weather—as well as logistical challenges—ruled out their hometowns. Then Kiri saw a magazine article about Beaulieu Vineyard and decided it would be the perfect place to get married. When she saw the grounds in person, the flowering shrubs, expanses of trees, and lush lawns reminded her of Cyprus, where her late mother and most of her relatives were from. The site chosen, wedding plans began in earnest.

Making decisions was easy: Beaulieu has an exclusive caterer and Doug and Kiri were immediately impressed with her food and her manner. There was also no agonizing over which florist to use. Kiri had seen a San Francisco florist's designs in a magazine and greatly admired his work, especially his French sensibility and adventurous style. Because weather in the Napa Valley is consistently good in August, they never considered tenting their reception—it would all be in the open air. Over the months of planning, Doug's mother and Kiri worked closely with the florist to take full advantage of the

The bride and her father.

setting, playing off the colors in the gardens while adding a little drama. They wanted the wedding to have a Mediterranean flavor, so the floral design included olive trees and other greenery from that region.

A series of recommendations led to the rest of the vendors the couple would hire. The caterer suggested the baker, who suggested the photographer, who suggested the hair and makeup team. Beaulieu provided the tables and chairs, while the caterer supplied everything for the tabletops. Except for hiring a band, Kiri and Doug had made all of the big decisions.

The planning continued in waves, with a few months of intense work followed by a lull. Researching and booking hotels in every price range consumed a lot of Kiri's time. Eight months before the wedding, the couple sent their guests a save-the-date packet with information about accommodations and things to do in Napa Valley.

By far the most stressful part of the planning was finding the right officiant and devising an interfaith ceremony that would incorporate elements of both their heritages. Kiri had grown up in the Greek Orthodox Church, which dictates that marriages be performed in a church and prohibits interfaith weddings; Doug is Jewish. After much trial and tribulation, Doug discovered that the rabbi from his hometown temple was going to be in Northern California on vacation the week they were getting married. He got in touch with the rabbi and explained the situation, and the rabbi agreed to officiate the interfaith service.

The bride had a very relaxing start to her wedding day. After breakfast at the hotel with her family, she had a massage. Soon after, the hair and makeup artists arrived. But at the last minute, Kiri decided against using the custom-made beaded headpiece she had planned on wearing. At her request, a friend went off in search of small white flowers for her hair. By the time she returned, they were running late, and Kiri arrived at Beaulieu just twenty minutes before the ceremony, still needing to dress. "That was a little stressful," she recalls.

His and her heritage:
A flowering huppah and
Greek wedding wreaths.

1. The bride in her embroidered
   corseted dress.
2. Parasols offer guests some
   welcome shade.

1.

It was a four o'clock ceremony, and the weather was warm. The property was a paradise of large trees, flowering shrubbery, and formal gardens. Guests walked over a bridge and on flower-lined paths to a patio where they could mingle and sip pomegranate lemonade.

The bride had made her quick change into an embroidered, corseted two-piece dress with an ivory-colored, satin fishtail skirt. The white flowers in her hair were visible through her long tulle veil. Her bouquet had a wildflower look, with russet and red roses and berries surrounded by olive branches and greenery. As Greek folk musicians played, she walked down one set of stone steps, escorted by her father, to meet Doug. Together the couple then walked up another set of stairs, these lined with cypress trees, to an organic huppah that was a botanical masterpiece. Its frame was made from manzanita (with camouflaged rebar for extra support), while the canopy was a mix of greenery and olive branches with some pomegranates—a symbol of fertility—for color. Guests sat below, shielding themselves from the August sun with white umbrellas provided by the couple.

The rabbi conducted a Jewish service that included an exchange of rings and vows. Then a close friend of Kiri's who had come from England stood at the huppah. In fluent Greek he read a traditional Greek Orthodox prayer—which he later translated—about a king and queen linked together with a ribbon who recite a prayer and exchange wreaths three times. As he spoke, the bride and groom performed the wreath ceremony. "Putting together this service was a kind of journey for us," says Kiri. "We realized the religious aspect wasn't so important, but we both wanted our cultures represented."

Greek folk music was struck up again during the cocktail hour following the ceremony. Bars were set up and decorated with simple pots of herbs and topiaries. Between the music and the scenery, the ambience was very Mediterranean, and Kiri's Greek relatives felt right at home.

A beautiful grove served as the dining area. Lights were strung in the trees and vines overhead. Gracing the tables were dramatic topiaries: a base of multicolored roses, herbs, berries, and greenery

2.

held a candelabra covered with moss and olive branches. After a meal set to jazz, guests were ready for dancing. To create a more inviting dance floor, the florist had framed it in hedges. As guests grooved to a band playing Motown classics, they could smell the heavenly scent of the fresh gardenias that had been tucked into the hedges.

To Doug and Kiri, the day was perfect. They just wished it could have lasted longer! The 10:00 P.M. music cutoff—the bane of all Napa Valley wedding partiers—came much too soon. It was a custom Kiri found hard to explain to her family. "I'm used to going to Greek weddings that go on until two o'clock," she says.

Planning her own nuptials had been a crash course in wedding customs for Kiri. With the help of the professionals she hired and the guidance of Doug's mother, she mixed and matched traditions— some American, some Jewish, and some Greek—to create a wedding that was uniquely hers and Doug's.

1. Husband and wife,
   hand-in-hand.
2. The guests begin to arrive.

3.

4.

3. **Dining under strings of light.**
4. **The wedding menu.**
5. **Guests enjoyed pomegranate lemonade before the ceremony.**
6. **Tiny flowers accent the bride's hair.**
7. **Olive branches and berries give Kiri's bouquet a wild flower look.**

7.

6.

5.

Elaborate candelabras add
drama to the tabletops.

Beyond Bouquets

The floral design of Kiri's and Doug's wedding helped to create the Mediterranean atmosphere they wanted. Boxwood hedges bordering the dance floor and the branch-laden huppah blended so seamlessly with the environment that many guests thought they were part of the landscape. And that's just what floral designer Thierry Chantrel had in mind. He offers the following suggestions for designing outdoor weddings:

- Go with the environment. You choose a space because it has a certain feel to it, so go with that feeling. I design the flowers and greenery to relate to the character of the setting.
- Even when the event is outdoors and the floral arrangements are wild looking, they still need to have a basic structure and design. Everything has to be well organized.
- Floral arrangements should have depth. From far away you get an overall feeling for them; then as you get closer you see more and more details, some half hidden.
- If you want a different look for a centerpiece, try using colorful fruits and vegetables, such as heirloom tomatoes, eggplant, and kale, which all go nicely with blackberry lilies. Farmers' markets are a good source.
- Use branches and greens not just as filler but as part of the structure of an arrangement. A piece of greenery can be as nice as a rose. You can also work with grasses and wheat for centerpieces.
- I like to put votive candles directly inside arrangements for a wonderful sparkling effect. Adding light to a flower gives it a really nice glow.
- Candles can also be used to underline the architecture of a building or the shape of a pool, or be run along steps or pathways to invite guests into a space.
- I shouldn't be saying this, but some outdoor spaces are so magnificent, you don't really need extra flowers.

1. **Kiri and Doug saunter into the reception area.**
2. **After months of planning, the bride and groom enjoy their wedding.**

−3−

Getting Back to Their Roots

A home wedding offers a sentimental start for couples, allowing them to connect to
the past while planning their future. Here, a New England family pitches in ...
a backyard Indian ceremony dates back centuries ... a hometown wedding draws on
all things familiar ... and the Old World meets the New on the isle of Capri.

Do-It-Yourself
Determination

Meredith Bennett & Robert LaForty

With its towering pine trees, ten-foot hedges, prize-winning garden, quintessential New England barn, and six acres stretching to the water's edge, Meredith Bennett had to look no farther than her own backyard (actually, her mother's and stepfather's) for the perfect setting for her wedding to Robert LaForty.

When their wedding day came, however, the weather was anything but perfect. All week it had rained, and that day was no exception. Hours before their nuptials, showers continuing, Meredith and Robert shifted into contingency mode. The ceremony—which was to have occurred in her mother's English garden—would be moved into a tent. Rather than a waterfront cocktail hour, drinks and hors d'oeuvres would be served in the barn. As planned, dinner and dancing would be held in the tent, but the caterers would now have to wait until after the ceremony to set up.

Robert and Meredith easily adopted a show-must-go-on attitude, but they couldn't help but be disappointed that after ten months of carefully choreographing every step of their wedding, they now had to settle for Plan B. Then, about an hour before the ceremony, there was a break in the rain. Should they chance going

Robert and Meredith have
their garden ceremony, under
a clear blue sky.

The bride was given away by her twin brother.

back to the original plan? Would the ground be too wet to walk on? Robert left the decision in the hands of his best man as he headed inside to shower and change. Half an hour later, sun breaking through the clouds, the groomsmen and catering staff, joined by some early guests, were lugging chairs and floral arrangements back out of the tent and down to the garden.

By the time Meredith was escorted down the aisle by her twin brother, the sun was shining and a drying breeze carried the mingled scents of flowers, salt water, and pine. At their seats, guests found wedding programs that included a Willa Cather quote: "Where there is great love, there are always miracles." As the bride and groom recited their vows, nature provided backup music in the form of wind whistling through the pines.

When the ceremony concluded, guests headed toward the old red barn, its massive doors open to a water view. With its beautiful wood siding and New England accents like hurricane lamps and fishing nets, it provided a charmingly rustic backdrop to the artistically displayed appetizers. Music floating down from speakers perched in the rafters added to the barn's atmosphere. Robert had taken some of the couple's favorite songs and put together a professional-quality mix (he also made tapes to play during the reception, whenever the band took a break). "Having the cocktail hour in the barn was something we hadn't originally planned on, but it was a great move," says Robert.

While the cocktail location was serendipitous, the wedding itself was the result of months of planning. From the outset, the couple wanted an outdoor celebration and they wanted to keep it fairly simple: "More fun than fancy," says Meredith.

While the couple worked on budgets and timelines, her parents looked over their property with a critical eye and started their own to-do list, which included painting the house, seeding the lawn, trimming the 100-foot pine trees that lined the driveway, and checking to see whether their electrical system could withstand the strain of generators and sound systems. In order to create the perfect spot for the ceremony, they had an opening cleared in the 150-foot-long hedges bordering the garden.

Knowing that you can never count on New England weather, the couple immediately decided to invest in a tent, renting one big enough to accommodate 165 guests. Before determining the flow of the wedding, they had to figure out the tent placement. "You don't

A fishing net gives the barn
a New England accent.

realize that a lawn really isn't flat until you try to find a place to set up a tent," says Robert. Fortunately, they found an area near the barn that was fairly even and close enough to the garage so the caterers could set up. They were able to angle the tent for an optimal view of the water. When it came to deciding where to put the band and dance floor and how to position the tables, the couple drew schematics, taking into consideration lighting, sound, and the natural movements of guests. In the do-it-yourself spirit of their wedding plans, Robert and his father-in-law-to-be built a riser for the band. The couple thought of everything, even lining the path to the portable bathrooms with candles in sand-filled bags.

For illumination, Robert and Meredith purchased strings of tiny white lights and dozens of Chinese lanterns to hang from the tent's ceiling. Robert also designed and built his own lighting grid, one that would hold forty-five lights at various heights. Deciding on a caterer was the next order of business. Most of the food they sampled was less than thrilling. Then a friend recommended two women fairly new to catering who offered a menu that departed from the traditional New England fare of meat, potatoes, and a vegetable. Their repertoire included Asian-inspired dishes that appealed to the couple and suited their plan for a buffet. Meredith and Robert ended up with a menu they loved that fit within their budget.

When it came to choosing floral arrangements and bouquets, Meredith had two experts she could rely on—the florist and her mother. "We wanted flowers that were either the same as or similar to those in my mother's garden," says Meredith. While her bouquet of roses, peonies, and freesia was white, the arrangements were filled with the bright colors—yellow, pink, and purple—that dominated the English-style garden. Because it was to play such a central part in the wedding, Meredith and Robert had a drawing of the garden on their invitations.

The last big piece of the wedding puzzle was choosing a band. The ten-piece band they hired included a horn section and kept guests dancing late into the night. As the party was winding down, everyone accompanied the couple to the waterfront and waved

A kerosene lamp warms
the hors d'oeuvre table.

farewell as they motored to a sailboat docked offshore, where they were spending their wedding night.

The family's personal touches and painstaking attention to detail added so much to the flavor of Meredith's and Robert's wedding, from the cocktail party music to the decorations on the wedding-night sailboat in view of the yard. One of Meredith's favorite items was the cake stand her stepfather made to hold nine different cakes. The day before the wedding, in between a family golf tournament and the rehearsal dinner at their favorite lobster shack, the bride and groom and her parents were still working on last-minute details. Meredith tied ribbons on programs and assembled favors, while Robert tweaked his lighting grid.

An at-home wedding gives you the utmost control over the event, but it creates a lot of extra work, concludes Robert. "Every weekend we made a five-hour drive to help get the place ready." In fact, a week before the wedding, the bride was painting her own white picket fence. The sixty-by-forty-foot fence that framed her mother's garden had been built—picket by picket—by her stepfather. "My parents are real New Englanders, who do everything themselves," says Meredith, acknowledging that without their extraordinary effort, the wedding wouldn't have been possible.

Aside from the stress of time-crunch details the bride and groom had to attend to, there's nothing they would change about their wedding. "Every time we go to her parents' house," says Robert, "we can stand in the same place where we got married and it brings back some great memories."

1. **Guests mingle in and around the barn.**
2. **A canning jar serves as candleholder.**
3. **Meredith and Robert walk hand-in-hand.**

5.

6.

4.

4. Seats decked out for the
   bride and groom.
5. A stand for nine wedding
   cakes, fashioned by
   Meredith's stepfather.
6. Edible decorations.

The bride and groom
framed by towering pines.

96

Home Improvement

"A lot of people think it will be easier and less expensive to have a home wedding, but really it's just as involved and probably more difficult to plan," says Meredith. Still, she adds, for couples willing to put in the effort, having a home wedding allows them the freedom to influence every detail. If you're thinking about a backyard reception, she suggests taking a good look at your budget and keeping in mind the following:

• Make sure the whole family is on board, since planning a home wedding will mean extra work and inconvenience for everyone.

• Take into account everything you might need to do to prepare your house and yard, such as touch-up painting, landscaping, and electrical upgrades, and include it in your wedding budget. Leave more than enough time to finish home projects before the wedding day.

• Decide at the outset whether you want guests in your house and, if you do, whether it will entail any redecorating. Be sure your bathrooms and septic system can accommodate the number of people on your guest list.

• Have a well-thought-out contingency plan for inclement weather.

• Consider parking options and decide whether you'll need to offer valet service. Another option is to have guests park at a nearby lot and provide shuttle service to and from the wedding.

• Decide where the catering staff will set up. If not in your kitchen, is there a garage or other indoor space, or will you need a cook tent?

• Check your home insurance policy—you may want to consider an upgrade.

• If you don't have a wedding planner, consider hiring a coordinator for the day, someone who can act as a liaison with the various vendors.

1.

1. **Evidence of pre-wedding showers.**
2. **The reception tent.**

2.

The Best of
Both Worlds

Shalu Narula & Hersh Saluja

Shalu Narula's and Hersh Saluja's wedding ceremony was like an elaborate play in two acts, complete with costume changes, intricate backdrops, and scripted lines. The couple, both born in India, opted for a traditional Punjabi ceremony performed in her parents' backyard. The following day at the Kohl Mansion outside San Francisco, with more guests and in different dress, the couple hosted an outdoor reception, California style. Between the two events there was one unifying theme: Morocco. "I've always been intrigued with that part of the world," the bride explains. "And I wanted my wedding to be a reflection of my love for that country's richness and colors."

On the afternoon of the first act, 150 guests were ushered into the Narula family backyard, which had been transformed into a treasure box of jewel tones. The picket fence that bordered the yard was camouflaged under pleated fabric, as was the deck. Colorful Moroccan lanterns hung from the porch. Hedges were draped with rich fabrics, and a bench was swathed in velvet. In the center of this brilliant scene were rows of chairs for family and friends. Many guests were clothed in traditional dress, which added to the bright tapestry of color. In front was a *mundup,* the wedding altar, with all of its ceremonial adornment. The entrance to the Narula home had been framed in garlands of marigolds, carnations, and roses.

The rituals began before the groom or the guests arrived, with just the bride's family participating in prayers, songs, and dance, as well as a traditional presentation of bracelets to the bride. After the ceremonial welcoming of the groom and his family, the couple and their parents proceeded to the *mundup*. Hersh wore traditional dress and turban, and Shalu—adorned with necklaces, bangles, shells, beads, and gold ornaments—was dressed in a magnificent red sari. While Indian music played, guests who were unfamiliar with the customs could follow along by reading from a beautifully designed program.

A priest led the couple through the wedding ritual, including an exchange of garlands. An hour and a half later, they were husband and wife. After a buffet of Indian food and more singing and dancing came the typically somber finale: as the bride prepared to drive off, leaving her family's home, relatives cried as they waved good-bye.

The following evening, the second act of their wedding had a mood that was purely celebratory and a guest list of 250. The grand rooms of the Kohl Mansion open onto a beautiful garden, where the outdoor reception was held. At the entrance, saffron- and burgundy-colored silk crepe waved in greeting to the guests. As they walked through the mansion to the terrace, they were enveloped in a Moroccan atmosphere created with luxurious fabrics, flowers, candles, and bowls filled with aromatic herbs and spices.

Upstairs, the bride and groom had a quiet meal together—they knew that once they joined the reception and started mingling with guests, they would not get a chance to eat. Both were dressed all in white, in outfits custom made for the occasion. Hersh wore a traditional *sherwani*, in an Indian paisley that matched the design on his wife's dress. Shalu wore a long-sleeved, brocaded bridal gown with a fitted bodice; deep scoop neck; low back; flared skirt; and side gathering suggestive of a sari. Affixed to the back of her swept-up hair was a simple tulle veil.

After their meal together, they descended the staircase, its banister wrapped in a garland of gold roses, past a chandelier covered with hundreds of deep red roses. Inside and out, the walls were draped with richly colored fabric. Sheer white banners hanging in front of the windows billowed in the breeze. The

Shalu and Hersh perform rituals that are part of a Punjabi wedding ceremony.

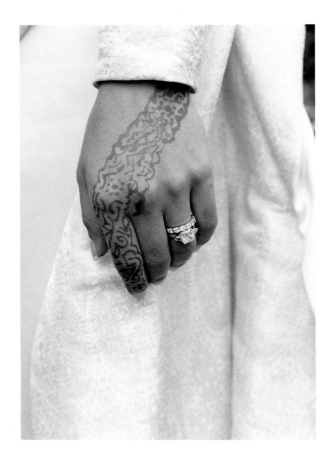

As tradition dictates, the
bride's hands are adorned
with henna.

Sparkling detail of a
guest's sari.

Moroccan influence continued in the courtyard with octagonal tables and seats topped with velvet pillows. Bowls of mangoes, lemons, figs, coconuts, and other fruits decorated the tables. Mounds of cinnamon bark and cloves spiced the air. There were heat lamps for warmth and candles in all colors.

In the spirit of multiculturalism (and because Shalu and Hersh liked the sound), a band played samba music during the cocktail hour. While the decor was Moroccan, the food was California fusion, on buffet stations set up in the courtyard. Guests could order a martini at the bar indoors or sample from the scotch bar in the library. Later in the evening, when it became downright chilly, the entire party moved indoors for dancing and dessert.

Shalu describes both days of her wedding as a fairy tale. And transforming her home and then the mansion into a marketplace of sensory treats did entail a little magic, plus the time, energy, and creative powers of a team of people. Choosing that team wisely, says Shalu, is the only way to attempt such an undertaking. "You're giving them a tremendous amount of responsibility. You need someone who listens to you and understands what you're saying. Someone who can take your vision and create your dream." To help pull off the two elaborate events, she enlisted the help of a good friend who is an event planner, as well as an event designer to help make the ambience just right.

If she had to do it all over again, there's nothing Shalu would change about her wedding celebrations, "nothing at all … except maybe come back as a guest."

The groom in traditional dress.

1. The handiwork of a henna artist.
2. Gifts for the bride and groom.
3. Flowers, fabric, spices, and other treasures decorate the Kohl mansion.
4. A bounty of fruit on display.
5. Delectable appetizers.

6.

7.

6. Candles flickered indoors
   and out.
7. Treats for all the senses.

105

1. The entrance to the Kohl
   Mansion, scene of the reception.
2. Hersh and Shalu dressed for the
   second day of festivities.

Atmospheric Conditions

Shalu's and Hersh's wedding and reception took place in two different locations, and each went through a transformation to provide the rich and textured atmosphere they were after. The mastermind of this metamorphosis was Grant Rector, a San Francisco event designer. Here, he shares his tips for setting the scene for an outdoor wedding:

- Candlelight, candlelight, candlelight. For an evening or nighttime event, you don't absolutely have to have flowers, but you do need candlelight. Not only does it set an intimate tone, it adds a lovely incandescent glow.
- Play up the beauty of your outdoor setting. If you choose the right location, nature will provide the decorations. But sometimes you need to help Mother Nature. We did that in the Narula yard by filling in the hedges with fabric.
- Draping fabric is a great way to diffuse light.
- Creating different areas within a space adds drama.
- By defining borders you can make a space more intimate. You can use furniture, fabric, or greenery.
- However you choose to decorate, keep it in scale with the space.
- Engage all the senses. Think about how things will look, feel, and smell. Scented candles, fragrant flowers, greenery, rich fabric, and soft pillows used together will create a layered quality that's rich and sensual.
- Decorate tables with herbs, spices, fruits, and vegetables for a nontraditional look.

Moroccan lanterns swing from the Narulas' porch.

107

Memory Lane

Whitney Walker & Lee Brown

When Whitney Walker was young, her grandfather would take her for strolls, stopping to point out the various types of trees that flourished in their lushly forested neighborhood. Those childhood walks instilled a deep appreciation in her for all things green, and her wedding reception was a testament to that love. But the verdant scenery wasn't the only reason she chose to hold her nuptials to Lee Brown in Lake Forest, near Chicago. She wanted to be married in a place that provided a deep sense of family, community, and familiarity.

An outdoor wedding in the Chicago area is always a gamble, but the couple tried to better their odds for a beautiful day. Summers are notoriously humid, and an early spring date means the threat of a late snowstorm, so Whitney and Lee decided the best bet, weather-wise, would be late May or early June. After eliminating holiday weekends, checking their calendars with key relatives, confirming the availability of the church and reception site, and consulting the *Farmers' Almanac,* they set the date: June 4.

From the outset, the couple planned their wedding with two watchwords: simplicity and sophistication. The wedding ceremony would be indoors at the Whitney family's church, the reception

Guests make themselves
comfortable during the
cocktail hour.

The bride and groom lead the way and the wedding party follows.

outdoors at a nearby country club. The spacious patio on the lower level of the clubhouse would serve as a cocktail area, and the sit-down dinner would be under a tent. While Whitney envisioned a beautifully clear and perfect wedding day, arrangements still had to include contingency plans, such as a tent with flooring (the last thing she wanted to worry about was spike heels sinking in damp ground) and flaps that could be rolled down in case of rain. A canopied walkway from the clubhouse to the reception area was another protective measure against precipitation. And in the event that the mercury dipped or soared, air conditioning and heating units were on standby. If the weather gods proved fickle, she also had the option of moving the cocktail hour inside to a wood-paneled room next to the patio. Although the room is beautiful, Whitney says she would have been disappointed if she had had to use it: "The dark wood wasn't the look I had in mind."

Whitney and her mother knew that thoughtful details make all the difference in personalizing a wedding. For table and menu cards, they selected a heavy stock in forest green with gold lettering. White silk organza tablecloths added another elegant touch to the overall setting. Striving to make their guests as comfortable as possible, they rented cushioned chairs rather than using the ones available at the club. And the menu centered on Whitney's favorite meal—filet mignon and French fries.

While Whitney and her mother took the lead in the wedding production, the groom-to-be got in on the act as well. He selected the groomsmen's tuxedos, classic cut with a French-blue bow tie. His taste in dessert was also incorporated into the plans. While the wedding cake was to be a traditional tiered white-on-white, adorned with gardenias, he would have a separate chocolate cake, decorated with a Weber grill and his monogram in icing. At his request, chocolate chip cookies and ice cream were also to be served. Together, he and Whitney auditioned the band and tasted wines until they found the perfect vintage.

In the end, the Walker-Brown nuptials strongly reflected the couple's style. The ceremony was very traditional, and the black-tie reception formal, but the outdoor setting kept it down to earth. Before and after dinner, elegantly dressed guests lounged on Adirondack chairs and children had the run of the grounds. And while almost 300 people attended, the wedding atmosphere was still somehow very intimate. "We didn't invite anyone we didn't have regular contact with," Whitney says. Since the bride and groom first met in high school and had shared a long history, most friends and relatives knew people from both sides of the aisle.

Whitney and Lee were married at a 6:00 P.M. ceremony by her godmother's husband, an Episcopal minister. The bride, wearing a strapless silk organza gown with clean lines and a full skirt, was escorted down the aisle by her father and grandfather. For her attendants' dresses she chose simple two-piece silk ensembles in a light shade of gray. Says Whitney: "It's sufficiently non-bridesmaidy, and since the church is a dark gray stone, I thought the dresses would be striking against that setting." The bride's bouquet was simple—white roses and greenery—while the bridesmaids carried a single type of flower, either white or pink, with no two bouquets the same. Once declared husband and wife, the couple and their attendants piled into an open-air trolley car for the two-mile ride through the center of Lake Forest to the reception.

While guests arrived, the wedding party stood on the perfectly manicured grounds of the country club among the towering elms and soaring hedges for a series of photographs. With clear skies; warm, early evening light; and just enough of a nip in the air to put the girls' pashmina wraps to good use, the day was picture-perfect.

Guests trickled into the club through an open courtyard onto a patio, where a bar was set up and appetizers were served. Conversation and laughter fronted a string quartet. Walking toward the patio, Whitney and Lee stopped to savor the scene. To one side, a splash of color, guests mingling against the red brick clubhouse, a lovely Greek Revival mansion. A few yards away, the dining area provided a contrasting picture. The large tent was white, its poles camouflaged with greenery and trees. The color scheme continued with tables dressed all in white, each with a topiary centerpiece containing gardenias and white roses. While the sides of the tent were open, a billowing white drapery closed off the back. To create a twinkling effect, lanterns and candles had been hung at different levels from the tent's ceiling. Later, as the evening grew dark, guests could almost believe they were in a tree grove looking up at a star-filled sky, exactly the illusion Whitney had hoped to create.

In planning the wedding, Whitney and Lee had kept in mind both ends of the multigenerational guest list (aged two to ninety-two). The tent was a short walk from the clubhouse, and dinner was served and the cake cut before the band was in full swing. The band itself was kept under wraps until the most opportune moment. After dinner, a billowy white curtain opened to reveal a dance floor and an eighteen-piece band with two vocalists. "It was my mother's idea," Whitney admits. "She loved the theatrics of suddenly opening the curtain and revealing the band and dance floor. At first I was skeptical, but I'm so happy we did it. It added a sense of drama to the occasion."

The clear delineation between dinner and dancing facilitated cross-table conversation and gave an easy exit to those who wanted to make it an early night. Once the band started playing, guests had the option of moving to a nearby patio, where surrounding trees were decked in white lights. Meanwhile, active children had plenty of space away from the reception area to run off excess energy while their parents danced the night away.

As if to signal the end of the party, sometime after midnight a light rain started. Before changing out of their wedding clothes, Whitney and Lee gathered family members and their bridal party, then the men and women separated and hit the locker rooms. Like teammates after a great game, the two groups recounted their favorite moments as they sipped champagne and nibbled on some cake and cookies. For Whitney and Lee, it was another chance to thank those who had done so much to make their wedding a success. "I'm so glad I trusted that instinct to go back home, someplace so familiar," says Whitney. "I just wish it had all gone by more slowly."

The bridesmaids form a huddle.

1. The wedding cake bedecked
   with flowers and candles.
2. A bouquet of lilies of the
   valley for a young attendant.
3. Tabletops dressed in green and
   white—the colors of the day.
4. Bride and groom walk the
   grounds.
5. The reception took place in
   a veritable garden of trees.
6. The scene that took Whitney's
   breath away.

3.

4.

5.

6.

The bride and groom steal
a few quiet moments for
themselves.

1. Each bridesmaid's bouquet
   featured a different flower.
2. The youngest member of the
   wedding party ...
3. And the oldest member,
   Whitney's grandmother.

Perfect Pitch

A tent can be a simple structure to protect wedding guests from the elements or the setting for an elaborately decorated fantasyland. Tents come in all sizes and in a variety of materials (some waterproof, some not) and can be set up on just about any flat surface. They can be white or colored, striped or solid, even clear—it's all a matter of preference and budget. If you will be using tents for the ceremony or reception, consider the following:

- Among the seemingly endless list of accoutrements from which to choose are archways, parquet floors, French doors, carpets, and light fixtures.
- Ceiling fans, air-conditioning units, and heaters are recommended for keeping the temperature inside comfortable.
- Multiple tents can be used for the ceremony, cocktails, reception, and dancing, as well as for foyer, kitchen, and rest-room areas.
- When determining the size of a tent, consider the use, the guest count, and whether or not there will be buffet tables, a dance floor, and a band. Generally, rental companies suggest allowing between fifteen and twenty square feet per person.
- When choosing a tent, decide how it will be decorated. Poles can be draped in fabric, covered with flowers or greenery, or camouflaged by trees.
- To create a warm and inviting ambience, the right lighting is key. Supplement candlelight with strings of tiny lights, paper lanterns, and pin lights. See page 75 for more lighting tips.

Marriage, Italian Style

Marisa May & David Bocognano

Since she was a little girl, Marisa May had dreamed about walking down the steps of the Santo Stefano church into the center square of Capri, dressed in her bridal gown, a handsome man on her arm. On her thirtieth birthday, that dream came true. She and David Bocognano descended the ancient steps into the piazza high above the bay of Naples. On one side, narrow alleys wound through the medieval quarter; on the other, breathtaking views of the rocky shoreline and a sparkling blue sea could be seen beyond limestone houses and lush greenery. It was another perfect day in Capri.

As they entered the square, the bride and groom were greeted by 375 guests from three continents, a band of Italian folk dancers and musicians, and a contingent of paparazzi and television cameras. Marisa's father, a native of Naples, owns one of New York City's finest restaurants. As Italy's unofficial ambassador of food and wine, he's a national celebrity, and Marisa's wedding was big news. "I felt like Princess Grace, walking down those steps with everyone watching," says the bride.

The center square was the setting for a public cocktail celebration. Tables draped in white linen and decorated with artfully arranged fruit had been set up to serve champagne and hors

An exuberant bride escorted
by her father.

Marisa's bridesmaids
step into line.

Santo Stefano Church,
the site of the ceremony.

Guests file into the church.

121

Bride and groom are greeted
by a band of Italian folk
musicians and dancers.

1. **Marisa takes delight in a Capri tradition.**
2. **A tambourine serves double duty as a holder for flower petals.**

1.

2.

d'oeuvres. Fashionably dressed guests, tourists in shorts, and locals in workaday clothing all drank to the couple. Meanwhile, the bride was hoisted upon a donkey, a Capri ritual to ensure fertility.

For Marisa, it was a homecoming. Although she lives in New York, where she was born, her family spent each August in Capri with relatives while she grew up. It was always a magical time for Marisa, and those summers provided some of her most cherished memories of her late mother.

From the beginning, Marisa wanted her wedding to be a blend of Italian and American customs. She and David were engaged a year and a half before the wedding (they got engaged on his thirtieth birthday), and within a few months the planning began in earnest. Marisa's father certainly knows how to host a party, and he worked with his daughter on every detail of the wedding. "I'm his only child, and this was something very special to my father," says Marisa.

In selecting a wedding gown, Marisa looked for a dress that was simple and suitable for Capri's warm climate. She chose an A-line silk-satin gown that was strapless and Empire waisted—definitely new world. For her veil, she turned to an Italian designer, who created a dramatic, long lace mantilla that added an old-world flair. She carried a bouquet of lilies of the valley, traditionally thought to bring good luck. While bridesmaids aren't customary in Italy, Marisa wanted to include close friends in the wedding. For her seven bridesmaids' attire, she selected knee-length champagne-colored dresses and matching miniature roses; the three flower girls were to be dressed in white.

Marisa and her father decided early on that the reception would be outdoors at the Palatium, a hotel owned by a family friend. After consulting with the bride-to-be, the owner herself arranged for the flowers and the band. Against the colorful Mediterranean setting, the floral arrangements would be all white with lots of greenery. The food, of course, had to be spectacular, so Marisa's father sent his executive chef to Capri to supervise the meal, which featured some of his restaurant's signature dishes. A contingent of local chefs collaborated to create the spectacular feast.

Many of the hotels on the island are owned by friends of the family, and a Capri-based relative acted as an unofficial travel agent, helping guests to book rooms and keeping track of arrival times. There were no glitches, and the guests who had never been to

Capri quickly fell in love with the Mediterranean paradise.

The Monday-evening wedding was the culmination of four days of festivities. Most guests had arrived by Friday, and each day a different family member or friend hosted everyone for cocktails, dinner, or brunch. With a French groom, an Italian-American bride, and a gathering of friends from all over the world, it was a multilingual, multicultural crowd.

After the champagne at the public square, some guests hopped on motor scooters; most of the rest descended by tram to the Hotel Palatium for the next portion of the celebration. Built into the side of a cliff, the red building offers magnificent views of the Bay of Naples and Mount Vesuvius. Below, on the rocky shoreline, a fleet of boats was moored, back from a day of fishing. A terrace off the building was the site of the extended cocktail hour. Tiki torches lined the space. A dinghy, set against a flowering stone wall, was filled with sea urchins and oysters and served as a raw bar. There was also a boatload of caviar.

The hotel's flourishing grounds provided a lush backdrop for the reception dinner. In keeping with the scenery, the tables, set around the pool, were decorated in white and green, and each chair slipcovered in stripes. Two dozen wreaths floated in the pool. Nearby buffet tables were adorned with intricately carved fruits and vegetables, a Capri tradition. Fresh calamari was fried to order on one table, while another held the artistry of several pastry chefs. In addition to a wedding cake and a birthday cake, there were some thirty different types of dessert. In between the seafood and the dessert, guests were served egg-yolk ravioli in truffle butter and rack of lamb. With each course, another spectacular wine was served. It was a culinary event to impress even the most refined gourmet.

As night fell, the scene was aglow in candlelight and, just inside the patio, the band was in full swing. The incredible food, magnificent scenery, music, and fragrant mix of flowers and salt water combined to create an intoxicating evening. As is traditional at Italian celebrations, guests received bonbonnières, five sugared almonds symbolizing health, wealth, happiness, long life, and fertility. People danced until 3:00 A.M., when the party moved to a nearby tavern

for more music and some singing by the father of the bride. The celebration finally ended after a meal of spaghetti at 8:00 A.M.

"I wanted something special and my father just put his whole heart and soul into this," says Marisa, who calls her wedding magical. She says that the day she had imagined since she was a little girl "was better than anything I could have ever dreamed."

The post-ceremony champagne party draws a big crowd.

The bride and groom
attract media attention.

A veil of tulle can't hide the bride's delight.

126

1. The cliffside reception offers spectacular views.
2. Elegant reception tables circle the hotel pool.
3. A monogrammed menu details the spectacular wedding feast.
4. The stylish groom.
5. The white floral arrangements contrast with the colorful surroundings.

2.

1.

5.

4.

3.

1. Guests enjoy cocktails
   on the terrace.
2. A Capri-style drumroll.

2.

Your Wedding Web Site

One of the ways Marisa and David kept far-flung friends and family members up to date on wedding plans was through their personalized Web site. Not only were they able to post helpful accommodation and travel information, they also included the weekend itinerary and local weather forecasts. Guests could log on to find out the proper attire for each event or read up on the history of Capri. Wedding Web sites can be a great way to give information to a lot of people at once, especially if it might be changing, such as the weather or last-minute additions to pre-wedding events. Some ideas for creating your own site:

• Decide how basic or elaborate you want it to be. Is it purely practical or do you want to include personal information? Some sites provide bios of the bride and groom, along with anecdotes about their first meeting, courtship history, and engagement. Some offer information about each member of the wedding party and their connection to the couple.

• Make sure all of the information you post is accurate and up to date (phone numbers, venue addresses, times of events, and so on). If something is liable to change, make a note of it on the site.

• Include maps and directions.

• Don't expect that everyone will see the site—if information is important, mail it out as well.

• Some couples include clips from songs that will be performed, a rundown of the wedding menu, and a copy of the program.

• A site can have interactive areas where guests can RSVP or send personal messages.

• Some couples even arrange a live Webcast of their wedding for guests who can't attend.

• After the vows have been exchanged and the honeymoon is over, relatives and friends can log back on to see wedding photos.

– 4 –

Going the Extra Mile

A weekend away with 100 or so family and friends ... These couples played travel agent,
tour guide, and host before taking their vows. The following destination weddings featured
rolling hills, beautiful gardens, dramatic vistas, and historic charm.

Love
Among the Ruins

Alexa Lange & Blaine Wesner

Rows of white-cushioned, bamboo-backed chairs were precisely arranged in a chapel-like space created from the ruins of an old winery. The ten-foot stone walls were lined with flowering greenery, the ground was carpeted with ivory rose petals and loose herbs, and clear blue sky stood in for a ceiling. Just behind the seating area, on either side of the aisle, stood a pair of iron arches covered with lush vines. At the base of each, billows of white and pale green hydrangeas, roses, tulips, lilacs, and orchids flowed from urns. Annadel Winery and Gardens—with thirty-five acres of rolling hills, rose gardens, and meticulously tended lawn—provided the spectacular setting for Alexa Lange's and Blaine Wesner's lavish but intimate wedding.

Alexa and Blaine planned every aspect of the ceremony and celebration together. The couple lives in Austin, Texas, but their friends and family are far-flung. Early in the planning stages, they decided that theirs would be a destination wedding. The Sonoma Valley, a place Alexa had fallen in love with during her college days at Stanford, seemed a natural choice. It was close to San Francisco, it offered lots of recreational options, and June weather there was consistently beautiful.

A friend told them about Annadel and after checking out the winery's Web site, they headed to Sonoma to see it for themselves. Annadel hosts only about ten events a year, so the couple couldn't believe their good luck when they were able to book the date they wanted. With the location and date secured, other details fell quickly into place. The florists, a brother-and-sister team, came with the site, and they worked together with the couple to create arrangements in shades of green and white to complement the environment.

The next step was choosing a caterer. It was to be a small wedding, only fifty guests, and Blaine and Alexa wanted the dinner to be especially memorable, so they hired a local company with a great reputation and settled on a six-course tasting menu that included seared foie gras, grilled quail, sea bass, and beef fillet. Blaine, a wine connoisseur, matched each course with a special vintage from his own collection.

With the wedding blueprint complete, Alexa concentrated on planning other weekend activities. "I'm very detail oriented and a perfectionist, but at some point, you have to decide you trust the professionals to do their jobs," she says. Becoming obsessed about every detail not only makes the planning very stressful, but, as she points out, "You lose sight of the big picture."

Guests arrived on Thursday for a long weekend of spectacular wedding festivities that included a vintner's buffet and Sunday brunch, with time for golf or spa treatments. The couple left welcome packages (arranged in a cowboy hat) that included some Texas treats, the weekend itinerary, and a "playbill" listing each guest and describing their connection to Blaine and Alexa in a few clever lines. That night at dinner, it proved to be an immediate icebreaker.

The day of the wedding, guests arrived by shuttle bus about half an hour before the 5:00 P.M. ceremony. By now they were a familiar bunch who settled into easy conversation as they mingled just outside the walled-in courtyard. Lemonade and iced tea were served, and a small table with art supplies was set up so friends and family could render their wedding wishes in watercolor. Guests were ushered to the site of the ceremony under a canopy of elm branches. As they settled into their seats, the conversations lowered to a reverent whisper. The courtyard was an intimate setting with an air of formality befitting the occasion.

A wedding program is accented by a pressed flower and a bow.

While the guests were arriving, Alexa, her maid of honor, and a few family members were getting decked out in the bridal cottage, a short walk from the ceremony site. The bride slipped into her strapless gown, which was fitted at the bodice, with a skirt that was slim to the body in front and full in back. The satin material made it traditional, yet it had a very modern cut and design. "It made me feel elegant—I didn't want to take it off," says Alexa. After the finishing touches to her hair and makeup, the bride was ready to make her entrance.

A string quartet played a different piece of classical music for each part of the processional. After the bride's and groom's parents had been escorted to their seats, the maid of honor, dressed in a sage-colored gown, proceeded down the aisle. Then, on her father's arm, the radiant bride slowly walked past row after row of family and friends, yards of tulle from her veil trailing behind. She carried a hand-tied bouquet of orchids, hydrangea clusters, roses, and sweet peas in shades of white, ivory, and pale green, colors that were echoed in all the wedding decorations. Behind the area where Blaine and Alexa stood, an expansive arrangement of hydrangeas, roses, tulips, and flowering branches filled a break in the stone wall.

Working with the officiating minister, Blaine and Alexa had designed a nondenominational service. A close friend gave a reading; the father of the groom, a Bible studies scholar, addressed the group; and the bride and groom offered a declaration of appreciation. The bride and groom performed a special wine ritual in which each alternated holding the wine glass as the other drank. The couple then recited the vows they had written, and the minister offered a closing prayer.

The quartet provided background music as guests moved into the cocktail area, where they were treated to caviar, an array of hors d'oeuvres, and vodka shots, as well as champagne, wine, and mixed drinks. Backed by the massive stone wall of the ruins, manicured lawns and hedges gave way to vineyards and a view of rolling hills and distant mountains. Guests relished the view, the convivial atmosphere, and the savory appetizers.

Beyond the cocktail area, a beautiful grassy site was set for dinner. As guests proceeded there, each found a glass vase holding a single calla lily with their name on it: a place card attached with decorative twine. The tables were dressed in white and silver hemstitched linens topped with elegant china. A silver Revere bowl filled with lush peonies, garden roses, hydrangeas, orchids, freesias, and sweet peas was centered on each table. Smaller silver dishes held floating gardenias. At each place setting, guests found cards describing the menu's six courses, as well as a wedding favor: cigars for the men and a bottle of Alexa's favorite face lotion for the women. Inside the sheer white package was a note of handwritten appreciation signed by both the bride and groom.

As afternoon turned to evening, there was a decided chill in the air, but with twelve portable heaters, guests remained comfortable. The chill also gave Alexa a chance to wear the coat she had had made to match her wedding dress. Once the cake was cut, a swing band got guests to their feet. They could have danced off the entire meal, if not for the 10:00 P.M. cutoff for amplified music (a county ordinance). The morning of the wedding, Alexa told herself, "Whatever goes wrong, it won't be because we didn't do everything we could to make the day perfect." And while she would have liked more time for dancing, Alexa the perfectionist admits that her wedding turned out pretty close to perfect.

1. **The couple exchanges vows.**
2. **Alexa and Blaine revel in the moment.**

1. A place card gets a
   floral embellishment.
2. A three-tiered feast
   for the eyes.
3. A gift for the bride
   and groom.
4. A table set for six courses.
5. The groom's place set
   with an after-dinner
   treat—a fine cigar.
6. A touch of Texas awaits
   each guest.

7. White and green orchids
   help decorate the bar table.
8. The bride and groom
   share a kiss before dinner.

1. The bride's bouquet, in soft
   green and white.
2. Alexa's veil and hair adorned
   with tiny white flowers.

1.

Dressing the Part

Knowing that hot afternoons give way to chilly evenings in the Sonoma Valley, Alexa had a coat made to cover her strapless wedding gown. It was chapel length, a simple silk chiffon design with long fluid sleeves, fitted at the body but flared at the back—the creation of Patti Flowers, in-house designer at the Stanley Korshak Bridal Salon in Dallas. "Even a little bit of a wind or chill can be uncomfortable when wearing a sleeveless, strapless dress," Patti says. She advises that brides and their attendants consider their cover-up options and offers these additional tips for wedding-day dressing:

- When choosing bridal and attendant attire, think about your wedding day as a painting and ask yourself what kind of picture you want to create. After all, your wedding photographs will last a lifetime.

- Before they select a gown, I advise brides to look at the portfolios of wedding photographers. It's amazing how easily you can see what works in pictures.

- Photographs tell a story, and sometimes it's the wrong story. If the mother of the groom, for instance, dresses in a color that clashes with the bridesmaids' dresses, it jumps off the page, and you're left to wonder whether that was an intentional statement on her part. Consult with both mothers and ask that they dress to complement the color palette you've chosen for the attendants' dresses.

- The bridesmaids should be dressed in colors that flatter the bride.

- Often brides see their body in a certain way and choose gowns to camouflage what they perceive as faults. That can lead to an unflattering silhouette. There are so many different styles that every bride should be able to find one that suits her body and the setting.

- Pay attention to necklines—the right shape will frame your face perfectly, and that's where the attention should be.

- The dress should reflect the bride's personality, so she feels natural in it. She—not the dress—should always be the focal point. If a bride feels too much like she's in a costume, she'll feel unnatural, and that will show in her face and the photographs.

Rain or Shine

Claude Kaplan & Michael Davies

Gaelic music announced the arrival of the bride and groom. Fiddlers gathered around Claude Kaplan and Michael Davies—two in front, two in back—and serenaded them from a quiet side street to the middle of a beautiful grassy field and their seats in the long white reception tent. As the musical parade approached, 200 guests cheered.

Like the wedding itself, the bride's dress, light organza and strapless, with very little ornamentation, was natural and elegant. She carried a bouquet of garden roses in deep pinks, oranges, and yellows, the bright colors of late summer. Claude had worked for six months to plan this day, and it took a few minutes before she could fully appreciate the scene she had created. "Seeing all those faces around us was stunning, the tent was beautiful, but it took a while for me to focus on everything."

Long, narrow tables were covered in muslin and topped with white linen table runners. Floral arrangements, in the same rich shades as the bride's bouquet, alternated with trios of chunky white candles in varying heights down the entire length of each table. Every guest was seated individually, so they could be introduced. This was "a Herculean task," the bride says, but one that paid off.

1. A reluctant ringbearer wheels
   his way down the aisle.
2. After a day of weather
   worries, the bride and groom
   have their garden ceremony.

1.

144

"Our wedding really was a coming together of Michael's and my worlds—many people had never met before."

Behind the head table, a ceiling-to-floor scrim, illuminated from behind, created a gauzy room divider. Throughout dinner, soft music wafted from the other side. Claude and Michael wanted to create an intimate meal, uninterrupted by dancing. "We didn't want the kind of dinner where everyone is up and down, dancing and smoking outside in between courses." Instead, they wanted a European-style sit-down dinner filled with personal toasts. By providing their guests the platform to speak (and letting them know ahead of time that was what they wanted), they had "the most astounding array of toasts that anyone has ever heard at a wedding," says the bride.

After the last speech, when dinner was complete, the curtain parted, theater style, to reveal the band, dance floor, and café tables. That, says Claude, sent guests the clear signal, "It's time to boogie!" And they did, with dancing and drinking until the police arrived at 12:30 A.M. Then the party continued where it had begun, down the street at the home of the bride's parents. It was a beautiful ending to a day that had started (literally) under a cloud.

Earlier that morning, the Kaplan house had been the crisis command center for all things weather-related, as the bride and her parents planned their strategy for dealing with weather that threatened to dampen (and possibly even soak) plans for the 4:30 P.M. garden ceremony. There had always been a rain contingency plan and they had a tent on hold, but when it looked like they would actually have to execute the backup plan, the bride resisted. They had already pushed the deadline for the decision from the evening before to the morning of, and now it was time for a summit.

The morning had dawned hazy and overcast, with an iffy forecast. But Claude very much wanted to be married outdoors, in a garden, with the sky—and not a tent—overhead. Her parents were valiantly trying to keep her happy, while dealing with the reality of the situation. They went back and forth with the tent company, discussing different scenarios. Why not set the tent up, but take it down at the last minute if the rain held off, they asked.

2.

Michael and Claude,
as husband and wife.

That wouldn't work, they were told; the company didn't have the staffing for a last-minute change of plans, and besides, they wouldn't want the garden to look like they had just pulled up stakes.

Down to the wire with the decision, Claude's mother came up with a plan to set up the tent in another part of the yard, allowing them to keep their options open. Her dad quickly found a spot on the opposite side of the house, away from the garden, that was large enough for a 200-person tent. Rather than having to shuttle chairs from one side of the yard to the other, the Kaplans rented a second set for the tent.

Claude tried to relax as she had her hair and makeup done. She was upstairs with her sisters and other bridesmaids. So far, the rain had held off. Her mother had prepared for the possibility of a drizzle by stocking up with 200 white umbrellas. At 4:20 P.M., the bride peeked out the window to see the first of the umbrellas opening. The rain had just begun. Her mother approached tentatively, afraid to break the news. But as if she could will away the rain, Claude said that she would have the garden wedding, and that the drizzling would stop. In the end, she got her way!

Just a few minutes after they were opened, the white umbrellas were folded and put away. Completely at ease, the stress of the day a distant memory, the bride walked down the garden aisle with her father at her side. The bridesmaids and a trio of three-year-olds preceded her. The ring bearer, her little cousin, had practiced his role perfectly the night before. The pillow bearing the rings was placed in a toddler-sized white wheelbarrow, and he pushed past about two rows of seats, then refused to go any farther until his mother joined him.

The bride and groom stood in front of their families and friends. They had each written vows, but not for public recitation. Instead, they exchanged them in letters delivered via emissary and read privately before the ceremony. Guests then shared Claude's and Michael's joy as they were pronounced husband and wife.

1. **Garlands embellish the porch railing.**
2. **Guests prepare themselves for the threat of rain.**

147

CLAUDE AND MICHAEL
August 24th, 2002

**ORGANIC HEIRLOOM TOMATOES
WITH FRESH MOZZARELLA**
Basil, Olive Oil and Sea Salt

**GRILLED STRIPED BASS
LEMON MINT DRESSING**
*Roast Potato Medley with Rosemary
Country Garden Corn with Lemon and Chives
French Beans and Balsamic Glazed Onions*

**WARM PEACHES, BLACKBERRIES
AND RASPBERRIES ON VANILLA ICE CREAM**
*Warm Chocolate Chip Cookies
Warm Oatmeal Lace Cookies
Handcrafted Chocolate Truffle Squares
Chocolate Caramels*

WEDDING CAKE

5.

4.

6.

1. The menu for the lavish
   wedding feast.
2. The bride's bouquet of
   garden roses.
3. Table arrangements pick
   up the muted colors of
   Claude's bouquet.
4. Michael and Claude,
   umbrella in tow, survey
   the scene.
5. The four-tiered chocolate
   wedding cake.
6. A stash of white umbrellas,
   just in case.

A gardenia for the groom.

Dining alfresco

It was the simplest of ideas, a wedding in a field. The execution, however, was anything but: "It took a lot to make it look so simple," says Cheryl Stair, co-owner of Art of Eating. For Claude's and Michael's wedding, the caterers had to have on-site ovens and a portable water supply. Here, a few thoughts from an expert on open-air dining:

- Outdoor weddings are the most complicated and usually the most expensive to cater. When hiring a caterer, make sure you ask a lot of very pointed questions so you start off with a true idea of the cost. How much extra tenting will be needed? Will the caterer have to bring in water or a stove, and is that included in the cost?
- A wedding involves so many different people—a florist, caterer, tent company, lighting—and they all have to work together. Wherever possible, hire a team or vendors who are used to working with one another. There's a certain comfort level and mutual respect that makes things smoother.

- Sometimes the weather factors into menu choices. Here, humidity is always an issue, so certain baked goods, like flat bread and meringue, don't hold up well. At Claude's and Michael's wedding, we served chocolate chip cookies, but we had to recrisp them in the oven on site.
- If you are holding the cocktail portion of the wedding in a different location, as Claude and Michael did, ask if the caterer will need to hire extra staff for setup.
- Unless you want your wedding to become a test kitchen, be sure to hire a company with experience catering outdoors.
- If you are holding the wedding in your backyard, be sure your home is equipped for the extra electrical needs.

The procession of bridesmaids.

A Lone Star Wedding

Margaret "Sam" Hamilton & Jennifer "Jen" Chaiken

Sam Hamilton and Jen Chaiken stood before 130 friends and family members for their wedding, the decor of which they described as "Mexican Shaker." They had all come to the Cibolo Creek Ranch, a luxurious oasis amidst the vast desert of the Big Bend area of Texas, for a weekend of celebration, culminating in this ceremony.

The dining room at Cibolo had been recast as a wedding chapel, the tables and chairs replaced with rows of benches. A ledge running along three sides of the room had been installed to accommodate some 100 white luminarias. The candles flickered, warming the adobe walls while playing light games against the rough-hewn ceiling. The couple stood in front of a wall of Belgian lace, backlit by candles, and under a huppah of white silk, elegant in its spareness. A cantor officiated at a ceremony that was highly personal but infused with Jewish tradition.

From the intimacy of the ceremony, the guests filed through a corridor of adobe buildings to open sky and a vista as big as all Texas. A cantina had been set up in a courtyard by the pool for hors d'oeuvres and margaritas. The cocktail hour also featured a mariachi band and the chance for life-size Polaroid portraits.

1. A lock is key for keeping the guest book open.
2. Sam and Jen's wedding program features their personalized logo.

1.

154

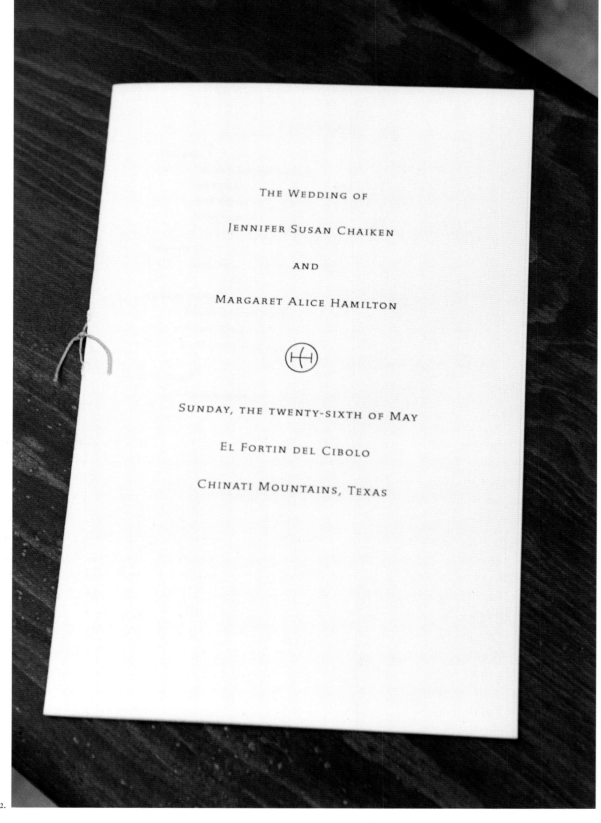

THE WEDDING OF

JENNIFER SUSAN CHAIKEN

AND

MARGARET ALICE HAMILTON

SUNDAY, THE TWENTY-SIXTH OF MAY

EL FORTIN DEL CIBOLO

CHINATI MOUNTAINS, TEXAS

2.

A member of the Mariachi band strums his guitar.

It was only after returning home from a friend's wedding in Sun Valley that the San Francisco couple began to think about making theirs a destination wedding. They were compiling lists of possible locations when a friend, an interior designer with impeccable taste, returned from a stay at the Cibolo Creek Ranch and suggested it as a possible wedding location. Upon visiting the ranch themselves, they were immediately impressed with the dramatic vistas, the lushness of the aquifer-fed gardens and orchards, and the Mexican-influenced architecture of the luxury resort.

But Cibolo had only seventeen guest rooms, so lodging was a concern. And Sam and Jen wondered whether the area offered enough interesting activities to fill a weekend itinerary. The ranch was a two-flight trip (and a two-hour drive from the nearest airport). If they were to ask guests to spend a full day just traveling, it had to be to a destination where they could spend a magical weekend.

Then the general manager of the ranch informed them that a nearby historic hotel had just reopened. It could accommodate the overflow of guests. He further chipped away at their doubts by outlining a variety of possible group activities. But it was after he made it clear that the staff of the ranch warmly welcomed the chance to host the wedding that the couple settled on Texas for their four-day celebration.

Rather than hiring a wedding coordinator, the couple hired a film producer Jen works with and enlisted the aid of their talented friends to help create the look of the wedding. Although the ranch's restaurant staff would provide the food, Jen and Sam hired an executive chef to help plan the menu and supervise the preparation.

Early in the planning stages, the couple sent out an elaborate save-the-date booklet, with enticing black-and-white photos, descriptions of the setting and activities, and hotel information. They were happily surprised when 130 guests from all over the country RSVPed yes. Over the course of a year, the couple and their team of friends planned a weekend that would foster bonding among strangers.

The kickoff to the weekend was a cowboy hat fitting. Each guest received one in black straw and then everyone assembled to have them custom fitted by the ranch's cowboys. Many guests wore their hats for the rest of their stay. One evening featured a barbecue with stargazing. Another evening, dance teachers were brought in so

1. The poolside cocktail area luminously framed.
2. Guests mingle outside the dining area.
3. The wedding cake, with alternating tiers of chocolate and banana.
4. Hurricane lanterns line the fort wall.

2.

3.

1.

4.

5. Wedding finery with a
   Texas accent.
6. Clay pots on display.

6.

157

1.

1. Flower petals mark the
   spot where Jen and Sam
   will sit.
2. Simple and elegant, the
   outdoor dining room.
3. The calla lilies pick up the
   tones of the ranch walls.
4. The guest book sits atop
   a rustic table.

2.

guests could brush up on their Texas two-step. Days were jam-packed with everything from rodeos to skeet shooting. The morning of the wedding featured a picnic brunch of bagels and cream cheese. By the reception, the wedding guests were like camp buddies at the end of a summer, basking in friendship and shared activities, and wistfully anticipating their good-byes. But not before an incredible evening of dinner and dancing.

The reception was a good example of elegant minimalism. The massive dark wood tables from the dining room that had been cleared for the ceremony were positioned in a horseshoe shape on an expanse of lawn. The four styles of chairs may have appeared arbitrarily placed at the tables, but in fact, a guest's entrée choice was signified by type of chair. The tables were topped with custom-made white runners, hurricane lamps, and arrangements of mango-colored calla lilies. The china, silverware, and glassware were simple but elegant, and the napkins were marked with Sam's and Jen's personalized logo. Inspired by the setting, looking like it might have been branded from a cattle iron, it was a circle with a sliver of a C intersected by a squat H.

One side of the dining area was bordered by the wall of El Fortin del Cibolo, a straight line of adobe reflecting the light of a changing sky. The foot of the fort's wall, all 300 feet of it, was lined with candles in hurricane lamps. Opposite the fort, a low stone wall was topped with white luminarias in rice paper sandbags.

The group dined on venison, quail, sea bass, and portobello mushrooms while the mariachi band played. It was a feast for the senses, combining gourmet food, the scents of flowers and sage, and breathtaking vistas. Depending on the direction of their gaze, guests had a view of the ranch's lush orchids, crimson plateaus, or distant mountains. It was the perfect setting for a lovingly planned wedding, and the happy guests topped off the weekend dancing the night away under a full moon.

3.

4.

Sam saddles up for a
photo opportunity.

160

Wagon wheels serve as reminders of the ranch's history.

1. Jen and Sam share a
   bouquet as they walk
   down the aisle.
2. A young guest armed with
   a basketful of flower petals.
3. A teepee for guests.

Guest Relations

When you take 100 or so people out of their element and mix them with strangers in a remote location, you'd better have a plan. Jen and Sam did, and here they share some tips on how to get guests mingling:

- Plan activities, particularly unusual ones, so people are experiencing things for the first time together.
- Definitely leave guests time to do their own thing, but have one or two group activities a day.
- Give your guests something they can wear or carry that signifies them as part of the group. The hats were particularly successful for us because you needed cover from the hot sun, most people didn't own their own cowboy hat, and a hat feels a bit costumey and funny but stylish enough so people don't feel silly.
- Make the first night a cocktail party. It's nice to have a low-key meet-and-greet on the first evening so that when activities start on the following day, people aren't shy about getting into the swing of things.
- Be sure your guests know what to expect ahead of time. We had plenty of surprises in store for them, but we did a couple of mailings that gave them lots of information about the area, descriptions of the weekend's activities, and a list of what they should bring.
- Give guests the opportunity to get into the spirit. For instance, we encouraged everyone to "pack their boots and buckles" to get ready for the barbecue, two-step dancing, and rodeo games. Consequently, everyone had fabulous cowboy attire and was able to really enjoy the events.

Cowboy boots, a Texas must.

Red, White &
Something Blue

Kerry Ferguson & Jon Walker

With its narrow, tree-lined streets and rose-covered cottages, Siasconset (known locally as Sconset), a historic village on Nantucket Island, served as the setting for Kerry Ferguson's and Jon Walker's September wedding. The Roman Catholic ceremony took place at the Siasconset Union Chapel, a nineteenth-century church with weathered shingles, multipaned windows, and white clapboard shutters. The historic charm was evident inside as well, in the white parson benches, wide-planked hardwood floors, and needlepoint kneelers.

Escorted by her father, the bride ascended the stone steps past a white railing wrapped with garlands and tied with satin ribbon, and waited at the wooden archway. She was dressed in a silk-satin form-fitting strapless dress and carried a bouquet of white roses. The bridesmaids wore knee-length A-line dresses tied at the waist with pink ribbons. Fittingly, the dresses were a pale version of Nantucket red (a color with a sun-bleached look). The women carried bouquets of hydrangeas that matched the French blue of the ties worn by Jon and his groomsmen. The flower girls, Jon's nieces, wore long white dresses with sashes that matched the bridesmaids' dresses.

165

The groom's nieces serve
as flower girls.

Because the chapel was holding back-to-back ceremonies, Kerry and the bride who would follow her down the aisle shared floral arrangements. At the end of each bench, a bunch of hydrangeas, stephanotis, and greenery was tied with a long white satin ribbon. Large arrangements of the same flowers sat on each side of the altar.

A violinist, cellist, and pianist had been playing classical music, but it was a trumpet that announced the bride. As she proceeded down the aisle, her cathedral-length tulle veil trailing behind, the trumpet solo gave way to the quartet of musicians. As if on cue, sun began streaming through the multicolored windows. The very touching ceremony was conducted by Jon's family priest and dedicated to his late stepmother.

For years the Walker family has summered on Nantucket, and now Jon had a house around the corner from the chapel. When he and Kerry had become engaged eight months earlier, they thought about eloping and later celebrating with family and friends with a big party on the beach. But, says Kerry, that was ruled out when she decided she really wanted to have her dad walk her down the aisle.

Although the couple lived in London, there was no question that they would have their wedding on Nantucket—they both loved the island and thought it would be the perfect setting for the casually elegant celebration they envisioned. They planned the wedding on their own (although they hired a coordinator for the day itself), which—thanks to e-mail—was surprisingly easy, considering that an ocean and five time zones separated them from Nantucket.

In March, they sent out save-the-date notices with information about transportation and hotels. By April they had most of the wedding plans worked out. Over the next few months, Kerry exchanged e-mails with a Nantucket woman who books musicians. The bride-to-be was very discerning about her selections, spending hours listening to classical music on the Web. She chose not only the pieces to be played, but also the arrangements. "I'd e-mail the versions of the songs I liked and the agent found the musicians to play them." After listening to tapes, the couple booked a cover band from nearby Martha's Vineyard for the reception. The last of the wedding details were nailed down in August while the couple was on Nantucket for a two-week vacation.

166

1. With her veil trailing, Kerry enters the historic chapel.
2. Decorations accent the chapel, both inside and out.
3. Flowers and greenery gathered in satin ribbon add a dash of color.

167

Jon and Kerry considered having a tented reception on the beach, but with the unpredictability of the island's weather, decided instead to hold it at the Nantucket Yacht Club. Its expansive lawns and docks would be perfect for an extended cocktail hour, and if it rained, the party could easily be moved inside. Plus, with a harborside location just a few cobblestoned blocks away from the center of town, it would be both scenic and convenient for guests staying at nearby inns.

While the reception site fell into place easily, reserving the church proved a little more difficult. There were already two weddings scheduled for the date they had chosen, and that, they were told, was the daily maximum on nuptials. After much back and forth with a chapel secretary and local merchants, the couple discovered the exception to the rule: a Sconset resident was entitled to schedule a wedding even if it was the third of the day. And since he owned a house in Sconset, Jon qualified. There was a catch, however—the latest available time they could schedule the wedding was 12:30 P.M.

Cocktails were scheduled for four o'clock, which left two and a half hours between the end of the ceremony and the beginning of the yacht club festivities. "We didn't want to have a lag time," says Kerry, so the couple scheduled tea at a nearby restaurant. "Since we live in England, we thought a tea would be fitting."

Once the wedding mass was over, 140 friends and family members filed out of the chapel and headed to a restaurant around the corner. It was a walk steeped in history. The old whaling village was first settled three centuries ago, and its weathered cottages, most with white picket fences and climbing roses, grew from the fishing shanties of centuries ago. After passing through a white trellis, guests entered a hedged-trimmed rose garden where they were served canapés and finger sandwiches. It was tea time.

After enjoying the snacks and tea, the wedding party drove through the narrow streets of Sconset in a Jeep caravan. In the lead car, perched on white wicker chairs in the back of the large Willys Jeep, the bride and groom sipped champagne. The motorcade headed toward the beach, and when one Jeep got stuck in the sand, the groomsmen in their navy suits (but minus their socks and shoes) managed to push it free.

After tea, guests were bused the eight miles into the town of Nantucket for the cocktail hour and reception. They mingled outdoors on the porch, lawn, and wharf, as three members of the reception band played. The water was sparkling, rough and white-capped from the wind, the remnant of a distant hurricane.

As the sun began to settle and the last bit of rose-tinged blue drained from the early fall sky, the revelers moved inside for a sit-down dinner featuring rack of lamb. Once the band began to play, couples began to wander onto the dance floor. The vocalists performed good impressions of the singers whose songs they covered, sounding like James Brown one minute, James Taylor the next.

The bride and groom dispensed with a wedding cake and instead had a brownie sundae station, which was a big hit with the crowd. At about ten o'clock, as the party was winding down, guests accompanied the couple to the dock, and the bride and groom got into a boat and sailed away.

Afterward, the couple said they were very happy they had planned the wedding themselves. "We like being in control of things," says Jon. But, they add, hiring someone to coordinate the day was crucial to their enjoyment. It allowed them to concentrate on enjoying the wedding they had worked so hard to plan. "It was absolutely beautiful," adds Kerry. "There was so much love in the room."

A post-ceremony walk past historic cottages.

A hedge-rimmed garden is the
ideal setting for afternoon tea.

1.

2.

1. Bridesmaids in their
   Nantucket red dresses.
2. A flower girl's simple white
   and blue bouquet.
3. A stack of missals.
4. At the back of the church,
   a basket of monogrammed
   wedding programs.

4.

3.

A Smooth Ride

When you hold your wedding on an island thirty-five miles out to sea, you might expect some travel glitches. The day before Jon's and Kerry's wedding, the fog rolled in and the airport was closed, so some twenty-five guests missed the rehearsal dinner. While getting to the island proved challenging for some, getting to the wedding activities was a breeze. Jon and Kerry had arranged buses to the rehearsal dinner, ceremony, and reception.

It proved a hassle-free and safe way for guests to travel from one end of the island to the other. Often transportation is an after-thought when planning a wedding, but leaving those details to the last minute means fewer options and more hassles. Some transportation tips:

- For the bride and groom, start by deciding your riding style. A limousine is traditional, while other options include horse-drawn carriage, vintage automobile, and trolley car. If you're a Mustang Sally, ride in a classic convertible. Let your wheels reflect your personality and the tone of the wedding. Kerry arrived at the chapel with her father in an old Rolls Royce; then she and Jon traveled through the village by Jeep and finally left the reception by boat. It was the perfect mix of traditional elegance and island casual.
- Next, decide how many vehicles you'll need for the wedding party and family. If you have many out-of-town guests or your reception site doesn't offer parking, consider renting buses or minivans to shuttle guests to and from festivities.
- Book cars early—begin investigating options months before the wedding. Limousine services are especially busy during the wedding-prom-graduation season.
- Most companies charge by the hour. Ask if there's a minimum or extra mileage costs. If you plan on having your rental car decked out with Just Married signs, ask about policies regarding vehicle decoration.
- Inspect vehicles before you book them and ask how the driver(s) will be dressed. Be sure to get a signed agreement outlining the dates, times, and locations of pickups.

The bride gets a lift from the groom.

171

Credits

Each of the outdoor weddings featured in this book had a team of creative people working behind the scenes to ensure the celebration went off without a hitch. If you are interested in their services, their contact information can be found below.

In Harmony with Nature

**Candace Brown &
Charles Nelson**
Pages 12–21

Band
Zydeco Flames
415 457 5767
zydecoflames.com

Bride's shoes
Anne Klein at Saks Fifth Avenue
212 753 4000
saksfifthavenue.com

Bridesmaids' dresses
Custom-made in Bangkok

Cake
Perfect Endings
707 259 0500
perfectendings.com

Calligraphy
Barbara Callow
Calligraphy
415 928 3303

Ceremony and reception
location
Beltane Ranch
707 833 4233
beltane.com

Dress
Badgley Mischka
212 921 1585

Eiffel Tower stand
Pottery Barn
800 922 5507
potterybarn.com

Flowers, lanterns
Kate Stanley Design
415 227 4547

Food
Alex's Catering
707 643 1711
alexscatering.com

Groom's suit
Hickey Freeman
212 826 3510
hickeyfreeman.com

Hair
Tony Marion of the Dream
Team
415 499 0422
thedreamteam.tv

Invitations, programs, menus
The Elizabeth Hubbell Custom
Letterpress & Design Studio
510 524 9898

Makeup
Chris MacDonald of the Dream
Team
415 499 0422
thedreamteam.tv

Rentals, tablecloths
Wine Country Party and Events
707 938 0712
winecountryparty.com

Terry cloth robe
Custom-made

Veil
Destiny's Bride
480 368 8868
destinysbride.com

Videographer
Thomas Hughes Video
Productions
415 925 8600
thomashughesvideo.com

Wedding planner
Everlasting Memories
707 795 7356
deemerz.com

**Julie Brown &
Dan de Serpa**
Pages 22–31

Accordion players
Tony Tomei
888 222 2772

Bride's shoes
Bridal Galleria
415 362 2277
bridalgalleria.com

Ceremony and cocktail
reception location
Ghost Ranch
505 685 4333

Champagne glasses
Waterford Crystal
212 532 5950
waterford.com

Decor
Carrie and Caroline Brown
707 433 1212

Dress and shawl
Michael Casey Couture
415 431 9550
michaelcaseycouture.com

Flowers
Vines
505 820 7770

Food for reception
The Old House Restaurant
505 988 4455
eldoradohotel.com

Groom's suit
Amelia at Neiman Marcus
415 362 3900
neimanmarcus.com

Hair, makeup
Julie Brown

**Francesca Vietor &
Mark Hertsgaard**
Pages 32–41

Band
Side Pocket
415 386 0935
sidepocketband.com

Bridesmaids' dresses
Nicole Miller
212 288 9779

Cake
Perfect Endings
707 259 0500
perfectendings.com

Calligraphy
Molly C. Malloney
415 924 1909

Flowers, metal buckets for
umbrellas, handmade sign,
basket with packages of seeds
Dragonfly Floral

707 433 3739
dragonflyfloral.com

Food, table linens, china
Taste Catering
415 550 6464
tastecatering.com

Groom's suit
Wilkes Bashford
415 986 4380

Guestbook
handmade by bride

Invitations
Janel Claire Design
510 601 6599
janelclaire.com

Lighting
Impact Lighting
510 232 5723
impactsf.com

Tent
HDO Productions
800 225 1471
hdotents.com

Wedding dress
Alencon
415 389 9408
alencon-bridal.com

Wedding planner
Kristi Amaroso Special Events
707 433 3739
kristiamarosospecialevents.com

**Madzy Besselaar &
Ian Taylor**
Pages 42–53

Band
Tony Bari Orchestra
441 236 1314

Bottles for programs
Gosling Brothers Ltd.
441 295 1123
blackseal.com

Bride's shoes
Charles David of California
212 767 0202
charlesdavid.com

Bridesmaids' dresses and
ring bearers' attire
Bergdorf Goodman
212 753 7300

Cake
Bernard Stemphlet
441 236 1431
stemphletscakes.com

China
Little Venice Catering
441 295 3050
diningbermuda.com

Decorations at beach
and huppa
Select Sites Group
441 292 9741
ssgbb.com

Dress and veil
Yumi Katsura
212 772 3760
yumikatsura.com

Flowergirls' dresses
Oilily
212 628 0100
oililyusa.com

Flowers
Suzan Sickling
441 295 3050

Food
Franz Wolman
441 299 5269

Hair and makeup
Strands
441 295 0935

Invitations
Euphorbia
609 896 4848
euphorbiashop.com

Lanterns
Pearl River Mart
212 219 8107
pearlriver.com

Menu
Pulp & Circumstances
441 292 9586
pulpandcircumstances.com

Programs
handmade by bride

Table linens
Cloth Connection
845 426 3500
clothconnection.com

Tent
Undercover Tent Rentals
441 296 0127

Setting the Stage

Alexandra Hynansky &
Gene Vados
Pages 56–65

Antique car
Father of the bride's personal
collection

Band
Joey Mills Orchestra
516 504 4400
stevenscott.com

Bridesmaids' dresses
Josephine Sasso
610 658 9022
josephinesasso.com

Cake
Margaret Braun
212 929 1582
margaretbraun.com

Calligraphy on favors
MJW Calligraphy
215 886 0135
mjwcalligraphy.com

Calligraphy on invitations,
placecards, JUST MARRIED sign
Bernard Maisner
212 477 6776

Dress, veil, and shoes
Vera Wang
212 628 3400
verawang.com

Flowers and lanterns
Yukie Yamamoto
302 658 8292

Food, champagne
Callahan Catering
212 327 1144
callahancatering.com

Groom's suit
Custom-made suit by Brioni
Boyds
215 564 9000
boydsphiladelphia.com

Hair, makeup
Stephen Knoll Ltd.
212 421 0100
stephenknoll.com

Invitations
Mrs. John L. Strong
212 838 3848

Lighting
Moore Events
610 518 3255
mooreevents.com

Rentals, tent
Events Unlimited
302 892 6105

Wedding planner, decor
Melissa Paul Ltd.
610 407 4270
melissapaul.com

Gina Cambre &
Storm Boswick
Pages 66–75

Bridesmaids' dresses
CALYPSO Christiane Celle
Shops
212 274 0449

Cake
Ann Boswick
902 423 7851

Calligraphy and invitations
Ellen Weldon Design
212 925 4483

China, table linens, and rentals
Tri-Serve Party Rentals
212 752 7661
triservepartyrentals.com

DJ
Samantha Ronson
917 693 2171

Dress, shoes
Vera Wang
212 628 3400
verawang.com

Flowers
Amagansett Flowers by Beth
631 267 2620

Food, champagne
Art of Eating
631 267 2411
hamptonsartofeating.com

Groom's attire
Emengildo Zegna
212 421 4488
zegna.com

Hair
Oscar Bond Salon
212 334 3777
oscarbondsalon.com

Lighting
Matt Murphy Event Lighting
631 287 7026
mattmurphyeventlighting.com

Makeup
Dawn Zarcone
718 980 1755

Rental furniture
Props for Today
212 244 9600
propsfortoday.com

Tent
PJ McBride Inc.
631 643 2848
pjmcbride.com

Videographer
Weddings by Two
917 601 8460
weddingsbytwo.com

Wedding planner
Jill Gordon Celebrate
631 324 2422
jillgordoncelebrate.com

Kiri Upsall &
Doug Miro
Pages 76–85

Band
Pride and Joy
415 383 2434
pridejoy.com

Bride's shoes
Jimmy Choo
212 593 0800
jimmychoo.com

Bridesmaids' dresses
Vera Wang at Barney's
NY/Beverly Hills
310 777 5792
barneys.com

Calligraphy, invitations, menus
Soolip
310 360 1512
soolip.com

Ceremony and reception
location
Beaulieu Gardens
707 963 5299

Cupcake tower
Perfect Endings
707 259 0500
perfectendings.com

Dress
Les Habitudes
310 273 2883
leshabitudes.com

Flowers
Thierry Chantrel for La Follia
415 391 0150
lafollia.ws

Food, champagne, parasols
Elaine Bell Catering
707 996 5226
elainebellcatering.com

Groom's tuxedo
Giorgio Armani
212 988 9191
giorgioarmani.com

Hair
Wallett Luburich at
Koko Represents
415 434 9007
koko-represents.com

Makeup
Wallett Lubrich at
Koko Represents
415 434 9007
koko-represents.com

Videographer
Thomas Hughes
Video Productions
415 925 8600
thomashughesvideo.com

Getting Back to Their Roots

Meredith Bennett &
Robert LaForty
Pages 88–97

Band
The Brian Walkey Band
617 421 9336
willowentertainment.com

Bride's shoes
Kenneth Cole
800 536 2653
kennethcole.com

Bridesmaids' dresses
Serafina
212 253 2724
serafina.com

Cake
Jacques Fine European Pastries
603 485 4035
jacquespastries.com

Cake stand
Durham Woodworks
603 868 7180

Calligraphy
Prelude
603 431 0694

Dress and veil
Pricilla of Boston
617 267 9070
pricillaofboston.com

Flowers
Katherine's Garden
207 363 8017

Food, champagne
Two Girls Catering
603 431 1863

Groom's attire
Brooks Brothers
212 682 8800
brooksbrothers.com

Invitations
Phineas Press
603 436 4402

Paper lanterns
Catalog for Living
800 950 7130
marthastewart.com

Rentals and tent
Exeter Rent-All
800 677 9838
exeterrent-all.com

Sign
handmade by Peter Dudley
401 521 4716

**Shalu Narula &
Hersh Saluja**
Pages 98–107

Band
Bill Hopkins Rock'in Orchestra
831 688 3700
hoprock.com

Bride's shoes
Badgley Mischka
212 921 1585

Cake
Masse's Pastries
510 649 1004
massespastries.com

Dress and veil
Alencon
415 389 9408
alencon-bridal.com

Flowers and decor
Grant & Co.
415 822 2101
grantandco.com

Food and champagne
Paula LeDuc
510 547 7825
paulaleduc.com

Groom's attire and shoes
Handmade in India

Reception location
Kohl Mansion "The Oaks"
650 992 4668
byreconly.com

Videographer
Thomas Hughes
Video Productions
415 925 8600
thomashughesvideo.com

Wedding planner
RSVP of Piedmont
510 547 8075

**Whitney Walker &
Lee Brown**
Pages 108–117

Band
Morris Ellis Orchestra
773 233 3044

Bridesmaids' dresses
Vera Wang
312 587 1700
verawang.com

Cake
A Piece of Cake
773 651 3300
apieceofcake.com

Calligraphy and invitations
jane weber, ink!
312 642 0747

China
Halls Rentals
847 929 2222

Dress
Vera Wang
312 587 1700
verawang.com

Flowergirl dress
Vera Wang
312 587 1700
verawang.com

Flowers
Gretchen Swisher
904 273 6062

Food, champagne
Owentsia Club
847 234 0120

Groom's attire
Ralph Lauren
212 606 2100
ralphlauren.com

Hair
Aydee
847 234 0037

Linens
BBJ Linen
847 329 8400
bbjlinen.com

Makeup
Allison Graf
847 323 4721

Tent
Partytime Productions
773 277 2600
partytimeproductions.com

Veil
Vera Wang
312 587 1700
verawang.com

**Marisa May &
David Bocognano**
Pages 118–129

Band at reception
Jerry Gennarelli of Capri

Band after ceremony
Scialapopolo-
folkloric band of Capri
caprionline.com/scialapopolo

Bonbonnières
Pratesi
212 689 3150
pratesi.com

Bridesmaids' dresses
Blue
212 228 7744

Calligraphy
Blacker & Kooby
212 369 8308

Dress
Romona Keveza
212 273 1113
romonakeveza.com

Food, champagne
Hotel Palatium with Chef Odette
Fada from San Domenico NY
212 265 5959
restaurant.com/
sandomenicony.com

Groom's attire
Custom-made by Duca
Italian Tailor
212 582 3225

Hair
Julian Farel of Julian Farel Salon
212 888 8988
julianfarel.com

Invitations
Papyrus Cards and Stationery
212 717 0002
papyrusonline.com

Reception location
Hotel Palatium
011 39 0818384111
hotelpalatium.it

Shoes
Peter Fox Shoes
212 431 7426
peterfox.com

Veil
Tia Mazza for Saks Fifth Avenue
Bridal Salon
212 940 2269
knog.com

Going the Extra Mile

**Alexa Lange &
Blaine Wesner**
Pages 132–141

Band
Jelly Roll at North Bay
Entertainment
707 224 0241
info@northbayentertainment.com

Cake
Perfect Endings
707 259 0500
perfectendings.com

Calligrapher
Martha Rasco Calligraphy
512 795 8668
respondez.net

Ceremony and reception
location
Annadel Winery
707 539 8478
annadel.com

Dress
Reem Acra at
Stanley Korshak Bridal
214 871 3611
stanleykorshak.com

Flowers
Sonoma Flower Company
707 539 2054

Food, table linens, china, heat
lamps, chairs
Paula LeDuc Fine Catering
510 547 7825
paulaleduc.com

Groom's suit
Palvileri at Keepers
512 302 3664
keepersclothing.com

Hair
Tony Marion of The Dream
Team
415 499 0422
thedreamteam.tv

Makeup
Chris McDonald of
The Dream Team
415 499 0422
thedreamteam.tv

Programs
handmade by the bride

Shoes
Fennaroli by Regalia at Stanley
Korshak Bridal
214 871 3611
stanleykorshak.com

Veil
Jennifer Leigh at Stanley
Korshak Bridal
214 871 3611
stanleykorshak.com

Videographer
Thomas Hughes
Video Productions
415 257 8636
thomashughesvideo.com

Wedding coat
Custom-made by Patti Flowers
at Stanley Korshak Bridal
214 871 3611
stanleykorshak.com

White gloves
Stanley Korshak Bridal
214 871 3611
stanleykorshak.com

Claude Kaplan &
Michael Davies
Pages 142–151

Band
Cal James Orchestra
212 768 0650
caljames.com

Cake
Kathy Burton Cakes
631 725 4614

Calligraphy and invitations
Kate's Paperie
212 941 9816
katespaperie.com

China, table linens, and rentals
Bermuda Party Rentals
631 324 7767

Dress and shoes
Vera Wang
212 628 3399
verawang.com

Flowergirls' and bridesmaids'
dresses
Serafina
212 253 2754
serafina.net

Flowers
Whitmore's Garden Shop
631 267 3182
whitmoresinc.com

Food, champagne
Art of Eating
631 267 2411
hamptonsartofeating.com

Hair and makeup
Hiroko Takada at Space Salon
212 647 8588

Lighting
Matt Murphy Event Lighting
631 287 7026
mattmurphyeventlighting.com

Tent
Nassau Tents
631 491 5507
nassautents.com

Umbrellas
White on White
212 288 0909

Margaret "Sam" Hamilton
& Jennifer "Jen" Chaiken
Pages 152–163

Ceremony and reception
location, food, cake
Cibilo Creek Ranch
915 229 3737
cibilocreekranch.com

Decor, art direction
Sam Hamilton and Mark
Cunningham
CHD
415 626 5489

Executive chef and food
coordinator
Larry Aleshire
larryaleshire@earthlink.net

Flowers
Fleurish
206 322 1602
fleurish.com

Hair and makeup
Chris McDonald of
the Dream Team
415 499 0422
thedreamteam.tv

Invitations
Black Dog
415 258 9663
blackdog.com

Jen's shirt
Roberto Cavalli at
Neiman Marcus
415 362 3900
neimanmarcus.com

Jen's evening pants
Badgley Mishka
212 921 1585

Jen's shoes
Seraglia at Fetish Shoes
415 409 7429

Mariachi band
Mariachi Aguila
915 333 9491

Programs and menu
Digital Engraving
415 252 9907
digitalengraving.com

Rentals
Classic Party Rentals
650 366 7951
classicpartyrentals.com

Sam's dress
J. Mendel at Bergdorf Goodman
212 753 7300

Sam's shoes
Manolo Blahnik
212 582 3007

Videographer
Bernard McWilliams
212 575 5478

Kerry Ferguson &
Jon Walker
Pages 164–171

Dress
Bob Evans
212 889 1999

Veil
Suzanne Millinery
212 593 3232
suzannemillinery.com

Bride's shoes
Jimmy Choo Shoes
212 593 0800
jimmychoo.com

Groom's suit
Anderson & Shepphard
011 44 2077341420

Flowers at church
Flowers on Chestnut
508 228 6007
flowersonchestnut.com

Bridal party flowers
Joyce Jaskula
508 228 0333
joycejaskula.com

Hair and makeup
Kimara Ahnert Makeup Studio
212 452 4252
kimara.com

Flowergirls' and bridesmaids'
dresses
Serafina NY
212 253 2754
serafina.net

Band
Sultons of Swing
508 627 3746
sultonsofswing.com

Reception location, food,
champagne
Nantucket Yacht Club
508 228 1400

Day of wedding planner
Carolyn Hills of
Nantucket Concierge
508 228 8400
nantucketconcierge.com

Invitations and calligraphy
The Papery
203 869 1888
thepapery.com

Flowers at reception
Sheila Duame
508 257 6371

Programs
Mount Street Printers and
Stationers
011 44 2074090303

Nantucket basket for
the programs
Four Winds Craft Guild
508 228 9623
sylviaantiques.com

Index